A Sketchbook of
Biblical Theology

A SKETCHBOOK
OF BIBLICAL
THEOLOGY

by

JOSEPH BLENKINSOPP

HERDER AND HERDER

1968

HERDER AND HERDER NEW YORK

232 Madison Avenue, New York, N.Y. 10016

Nihil obstat: Lionel Swain, Censor Librorum
Imprimatur: ✛ Patrick Casey, Auxiliary Bishop of Westminster
February 27, 1968

Library of Congress Catalog Card Number: 68–29885
© 1968 by Joseph Blenkinsopp
Manufactured in the United States

Contents

Foreword

THE RAPIDITY of change in religious thinking today has rendered conventional apologetics and catechetics obsolete, leaving the individual Christian to fend for himself. Of course the Churches still play some kind of supportive role in the practical living out of one's Christian life, but the adult Church member whose Christianity is still somehow an integral part of his thinking now realizes that he has to find his own way. If he is going to think in a Christian way at all, this will involve asking questions of the Scriptures and testing the scriptural area of meaning – especially as it comes to him in the form of Church doctrine – against his own experience.

The collection of mostly very short essays that follows has the purpose of providing some *foci* for discussion, some avenues of approach to the creative area of thinking to which the Christian scriptures are an invitation. It will be obvious that they are addressed, in the first place, to Roman Catholics; in fact all of the essays, with the exception of four, have appeared in Roman Catholic publications. In many ways the situation of the educated Roman Catholic is more difficult today than that of the educated Christian in any other confession. Not only does he experience the supportive role of the institution on the whole much less than Christians in other Churches; his personal appropriation of a biblically Christian position is made more difficult by uncertainty as to how biblical he can be while still remaining within his own Church tradition. The first essay examines some aspects of the history behind this present ambiguity and the second finds evidence of it in the Constitution on Divine Revelation of Vatican II.

Having made this point, I should hasten to add that these

short sketches are offered to the Christian of any or no particular affiliation who is looking for new avenues of approach to the Scriptures. As the title suggests, they are offered as thumb-nail sketches, not as a systematic survey of biblical thought. There is no particular order and no one criterion of selection of topic. My justification for putting under one cover pieces most of which have appeared in reviews is that several of them have provided a useful basis for discussion among groups meeting in universities, colleges and private houses. My hope is that this form of small-group discussion may grow and eventually become the standard way of searching the Scriptures and working out the meaning of our Christian commitment together.

I have to thank the editor of *Clergy Review* for permission to reprint essays III, IV, VII, X, XI, XIV–XIX; of the *Catholic Biblical Quarterly* for essay I; of *The Bible Today* for essay VI. Essays XII and XIII appeared in *The Life of the Spirit* now incorporated in *New Blackfriars*. In most cases I have taken the opportunity of revising the original piece where this seemed opportune.

I

What is Biblical Theology?

QUITE A LOT of discussion went on before and during the Council, some of it not at a very high level, on the relations between the dogmatic theologian and the exegete, the nature of the task each has to do, the limits within which each has to work and the desirability and possibility of a further *rapprochement*. The tension which this kind of discussion reveals is not, of course, new. One thinks, for example, of Bossuet's opposition to Richard Simon culminating in the latter's work being put on the Index, or of Billot, Lagrange, Hummelhauer and others during the troubled times of *La Question Biblique* in the early years of the century. Is it just a case of different mental habits, too much rigidity on one side and imprudence on the other, or of a lack of collaboration on the practical level of method and didactic? Or does it go deeper than this?

Both dogmatic theologian and exegete have had to re-examine the presuppositions on which they work as a result of the renewed understanding of revelation which is available today and which is to some extent reflected in the constitution *Dei Verbum*. They have also been impelled to dig deeper by the pressing need for a pastorally orientated theology and by the increased awareness of the problems of linguistic communication involved. The dogmatic theologian is or should be now aware that a structure and formulation adequate for the static world of the thirteenth century or the equally static if highly combative world of the sixteenth is no longer adequate for the twentieth. The exegete is or should be now aware that biblical language which is in general archaic and often mythical cannot just be thrown at people today. There is therefore the need for rethinking and restatement.

The current assumption today is that the only kind of viable pastoral theology is biblical theology. But at once a misgiving arises. The term "biblical theology" is not traditional in the Church. It was imported from outside, being first used, as far as we know, by Haymann in his *Biblische Theologie* published in 1708. Haymann was a German Evangelical of the early Enlightenment, and the whole idea of biblical theology as independent of dogmatics, that is, a system of Church doctrine imposed from above, compliance with which is enforced with sanctions, is the child of the eighteenth-century *Aufklärung*. It owed a great deal to Johannes Semler, one of the founders of theological liberalism, who had exchanged the Lutheran pietism of his early years for a rationalist and liberal theology with a new hermeneutics to match. The lessons taught by Semler were well conned by Gabler who laid down the basic principles of the new discipline in his famous inaugural lecture of 1787 entitled significantly *De Iusto Discrimine Theologiae Biblicae et Dogmaticae*. With this work biblical theology was launched as a historical science in search of a biblical truth independent of Church doctrine. Soon after we have the first Old Testament and New Testament theologies of the kind still appearing regularly today.

The practitioners of this new science were under no illusions as to the theological presuppositions of their work. One of the earliest and most influential of this school, H. Schultz, author of an *Old Testament Theology* still well worth reading, wrote as follows:

> In a description of this progress, the one really instructive fact is this, that it was only through the gradual giving up of the conviction as to the perfect harmony between the teaching of the Bible and the Church that this science of ours could obtain a start and acquire a position of growing importance.[1]

According to this way of thinking, systematic or dogmatic theology expresses the self-consciousness of the Church at a given moment of history, but this self-consciousness is shown by positive research backed up by techniques growing in resources and mastery from year to year to be not self-evidently identical with biblical truth. What would happen, for example, to dogmas

[1] H. Schultz, *Old Testament Theology*, Edinburgh 1892,[4] I, 79.

such as the Immaculate Conception or the Assumption of Mary when exposed to a biblical theology of this kind? The chief difficulty for Catholic theology here would be the implication of a severance between Bible and Tradition with the latter subordinated to the former. The Catholic exegete cannot take the Bible as a closed system. The fact that even before he opens it he has accepted a certain hermeneutical position, at least in the broadest lines, implicates him in theological *praesupposita* differing from those referred to above. Another prior consideration is that of canonicity. What this means in practice can be seen in Oscar Cullmann's thesis that the immortality of the soul is not biblical doctrine.[2] The *loci* adduced in theological textbooks to prove the immortality of the soul (in *De Deo Creante et Elevante*) include two from the Old Testament, one of which (Wis. 2.23) is canonical only for Roman Catholics, and the other (Ec. 12.7) of doubtful relevance. There is also the problem of natural revelation and natural theology. Though strictly speaking this forms only a prolegomenon to theology properly so called, its intimate relation to biblical revelation is not always worked out and its negation in a theology of Barthian inspiration creates profound cleavages on every subject touched on.

The type of theological thinking represented by Schultz is therefore repudiated on the Catholic side. At the same time, the debt of Catholic theologians and exegetes to biblical theologies written in this tradition is well known. Here we should recall that for a long time at the beginning of this century biblical theology as such, and especially Old Testament theology, was under a cloud, creating a discontinuity with earlier efforts. With the ascendancy of the Comparative Religion school it was felt impossible to sort out specifically Old Testament ideas from their religious background, and a general scepticism set in as to whether one could speak of an Old Testament theology at all. This period came to an end with König's *Theologie* published in 1922. Since then there has been a steady stream of "theologies", the most influential being those of Eichrodt and von Rad.

---

[2] O. Cullmann, *Immortalité de l'âme ou Résurrection des Morts? Le Témoignage du Nouveau Testament*, Paris 1956.

It is possible that some Roman Catholic exegetes have not thought out sufficiently the implications of the term "biblical theology" in making use of the various categories of biblical theologians writing in a different Christian tradition. This is particularly true, one suspects, of the use made of von Rad's writings which are not so favourable to the scheme of sacred history as is sometimes thought.[3] What this shows up, at any rate, is how intimately the mutual misunderstanding between dogmatic theologian and exegete is bound up with the Scripture–Tradition question which was left basically unsolved in the constitution on Revelation of Vatican II.[4] The exegete has to make sure that the biblical theology which he talks about and towards which he contributes is seen as the first stage, the decisive stage certainly, of a Christian theology which leaves room for the homogeneous development of doctrine. That is, his exposition has to remain open-ended, unlike that of the early practitioners of biblical theology in the German Evangelical tradition.

When, on the other hand, the exegete surveys the dogmatic theology as usually expounded up to recent times he could be forgiven for supposing that its unexpressed assumption is that the Church has had all the time she needs to extract from the Scriptures the essential propositions to which assent must be made and that, once the theses have been drawn up, the Bible can be left on one side. This would leave no room for that life-giving dialogue between the Word of God, *which is still being spoken,* and the community of believers. With the reassertion of the dialogue-character of revelation we may hope that the unreal dichotomy will be gradually superseded.

*   *   *

How did the difference of approach first come about? The first explanation to suggest itself is that the two disciplines have simply grown apart. In the high period of scholasticism, as long as it remained true to its original inspiration and structure, such

---

[3] See his *Theology of the Old Testament,* London, I, 1957; II, 1960.
[4] See below pp. 24 ff.

a tension was absent. This gives us a vital clue. Theology, if it is not to degenerate into a kind of celestial geometry or into byzantinism, must stay close to the *sacra pagina*. This has been put very well by Piet Fransen:

> A theologian who unconsciously tends to equate his own thoughts with the divine reality is not a theologian at all. He may be a very learned man, and clever, and almost indecently intelligent. He is not a theologian. Theological thought remains essentially a *diakonia*, a ministry of the divine Word.[5]

The delicate relation and balance between the Word and the human elaborations built on it is the touchstone of the precision and vigour of the Christian thinking of any age. Bonaventure put the relationship very well: "Theology is one science . . . its subject-matter, as contained in the canonical books, is the credible as such; as contained in the books of the commentators, the credible as intelligible."[6] This was also the basic conviction of Aquinas who is often condemned for having substituted a *Konklusionstheologie* for one of biblical inspiration by people who leave out of account his excellent biblical commentaries and forget that his principal job as *magister* was biblical exposition.

At the same time we have to admit that the scholastic method contained elements which made deviation too easy. The passage from *lectio* to *quaestio* and from *quaestio* to *disputatio* no doubt came about in answer to real academic needs but there was no lack of complaint at the time that the *disputatio* had brought with it a real shift in emphasis. Originally limited to questions not defined as of faith, it came in time to embrace all doctrine, and in so doing imposed on the Scriptures alien categories. Thus the *Summa* of Aquinas uses Aristotle and Pseudo-Dionysius as authorities alongside the Church Fathers and the Scriptures in a way which sometimes makes it difficult to see what the privileged position of the Scriptures is thought to be. What is fascinating in the decline of scholasticism towards the end of the Middle Ages is the intimate relation between the break-up of the patristic syn-

---

[5] "Three Ways of Dogmatic Thought," in *Heythrop Journal*, 4 (1963), 20.
[6] *Breviloquium* I, 1, 4 quoted in G. H. Tavard, *Holy Writ or Holy Church*, London, 1959, 20.

thesis of Bible and Tradition and the decreasing importance given to Scripture in the overall theological synthesis, a process hastened by the conciliar movement and the exaggerated lines of defence taken by canonists in favour of papal authority. This has a close causal connection with the structure of theological presentation: Church doctrine as taught by the Pope and other organs of the *magisterium* is proved by recourse to authorities of which Scripture is one. There is also a general lack of care in the interpretation of texts, often giving the impression that, since the point has already been authoritatively established on other grounds, scriptural interpretation was really a work of supererogation.[7]

As yet, however, there is no *argumentum ex sacra scriptura* and only a few of the elements which will go to make up the modern textbook-presentation are detectable. The "argument from Scripture" really has its origin in the sixteenth century, around the time of the Council of Trent, and mostly as an answer to the needs of controversy either Catholic *v.* Protestant or, within the Catholic Church, Jesuit *v.* Dominican, the latter particularly in the *de auxiliis* controversy. It is hardly a coincidence that this period saw the Bible divided up into verses, evidently for the purpose of providing ready-made ammunition for controversial ends. In this development of what has been the standard methodology up till recently the *De Locis Theologicis* of Melchior Cano holds a place of great importance. Published posthumously (1563), this work summarizes the teaching of the brilliant Spanish Dominican over several decades. Following this method, the theologian's task is to ask precise questions of the Scriptures, questions formulated according to a preconceived scheme, then find the *loci* which can provide an answer, then dispose of the objections. Cano lists ten authorities to which appeal may be made. He does, of course, hierarchize them to some extent and in theory retains the privileged place of the Scriptures, but it is not so easy for us

---

[7] The consequences of the break-up of the patristic synthesis for the position of Scripture within theology are clearly stated by Tavard, see note 6. He summarizes: "Once separated, each of them is maimed: the Church becomes a mere human organization (add, and theology a mere human creation); Scripture a mere book. The former falls into the hands of administrators, the latter into those of philologians" (p. 41).

today to discover the exact *rationale* of his methods. The authorities are: the Scriptures, tradition, the Catholic Church, councils, the Roman Church, the Fathers, scholastic theologians, reason, philosophy, history. It is easy now to see the distance which has been travelled since the high period of scholasticism in which theology started from the *sacra pagina* and was, so to speak, written in the margins of the Scriptures, a meditation growing out of an assiduous listening to the Word of God. What a study of Cano can show us is how our formulation of the Sources of Revelation (to use a dated terminology) must be reflected in the structuring of theological thinking, leaving room for a fuller incorporation of the dynamic idea of the development of doctrine, away from the basically apologetic and polemical model which characterized the period of Trent and the Counter-Reformation.

Modern Scripture studies have shown us the importance of development within Scripture, and in the light of this it is simply impossible to accept as probative many arguments formerly adduced, arguments which were based on an exegetical method which isolated and absolutized individual texts. What happens, for example, to the arguments adduced from Scripture during the Middle Ages to support the doctrine of the character of the sacrament of order? After all, this doctrine is medieval and can be traced back no further than Augustine and then only in embryo. Can we accept them today in the same way as they were expounded then? There is also the question of different "theologies" within Scripture itself. In elaborating a Christian theology account would have to be taken, for example, of the contribution of Deuteronomy and the Deuteronomist Corpus, the theological implications of Synoptic editorial activity, the contribution of *Hebrews* as distinct from the Pauline corpus. There is also the way in which the Old Testament is used. There is no place in the received model for a tractate *de veteri testamento*, one which would see it as a definite stage of redemptive history. Man is considered *in statu iustitiae primitivae* and *in statu lapso* but not *sub promissione*. Thus in writers like Anselm, Peter Lombard and even Aquinas there emerges no clear idea of the relation between the testaments, and Old Testament texts are often used – for example, with regard to

Christian ministry, priesthood and sacrifice – as if they had an absolute static validity of their own.

What is conspicuously absent in much medieval and Counter-Reformation theological thinking is the consciousness of history. We see Scripture today as the record of one saving divine activity, of the divine invitation and the human response, all leading up to the creation of a new reality in Christ. This implies that our positioning as part of this prophetic continuum, in relation to a definite stage of that history in the eschatological aeon of the Church, must in some way determine the way we think theologically. For example, in the treatise *de virtutibus* – and in normal theology in general – we can ask whether it is legitimate just to categorize the virtues in the style of the Nichomachean Ethics or even the Stoic catalogues, leaving out of account our critical relationship to the last aeon of salvation history, the one in which we live (see, for example, 1 Cor. 7.25–31; 2 Pet. 3).

*　　　*　　　*

I would like to go on to illustrate by examples the difference in method, approach and results between the received model of systematic theology and that of biblical theology. The first is the treatment of the passion and death of Jesus. In the textbooks still in use in seminaries this is generally set out in seven theses which are based on three of the twelve articles on the subject in the *Summa* of St. Thomas Aquinas.[8] The doctrine is articulated by means of three categories: satisfaction, meritorious causality, redemption. The first is canonized by its use in the Council of Trent (session 6, chapter 7),[9] but an explicit doctrine of satisfaction goes back no further than Anselm in whose writings it appears as a metaphor drawn from the social life of that time. The term itself is neither biblical nor patristic. The fact that the opening

---

[8] A recent example of the textbook treatment is found in the *Sacrae Theologiae Summa* of the edition B.A.C. (Biblioteca de Autores Cristianos), Madrid, 1956. It is of recent date, typical in layout and approach and still used extensively in seminaries. See for this question III, 243–315.

[9] Denz. 799.

thesis on the Passion is occupied with the Thomist–Scotist dispute on condign satisfaction would already suggest a serious lack of a sense of proportion.

The second category brings us up against a similar difficulty since, as the textbooks at once make clear, the idea of meritorious causality is found neither in the Fathers nor in Scripture. It drives a wedge between the Passion and the Resurrection since Jesus could not have merited by the latter, and therefore makes it impossible to see the Resurrection as a mystery of salvation for men. The way of speaking in the New Testament, especially in the kerygmatic sermons in Acts, suggest that somehow death and resurrection are one event: "whom you crucified . . . but God raised him up" (Acts 2.23–4), "they put him to death . . . but God raised him on the third day" (Acts 10.39–40). Biblically, the Resurrection is the climax of saving history; he who raised Jesus is none other than "the God of Abraham, Isaac and Jacob, the God of our fathers" (Acts 3.13). In the textbooks some of these positive elements are mentioned, but they are usually crowded into a scholion to the thesis on the death of Jesus as redemptive. In the *Summa* there are two articles on the Resurrection as the cause of our resurrection and justification. With his usual insight St Thomas moved from meritorious to efficient causality in dealing with the Resurrection, as indeed he had to. Biblical theology restores the unity of the one death-to-life event thereby restoring the meaning which it had in the New Testament.

The third category, that of redemption, is dealt with in two articles in the *Summa* (qu. 48, art. 4 and 5) and here the theology is set in the mould of payment, the payment of a price, as is particularly clear from the *respondeo* of art. 5. In the thesis treatment of redemption there are, again, many positive elements: *luo, lutron* and related forms are given their biblical meaning, the practice of sacral manumission is appealed to in the explanation of texts where the verb *agorazo* occurs, yet there remains the same impression of a lack of organicity. It never seems to get off the ground. A theologically organic biblical interpretation would suggest one development which would undoubtedly benefit the whole treatise, starting from the interpretation of the verb

B

ga'al and its present participle *go'el*, "redeemer". Where the text-books quote only isolated cases from Old Testament penal legislation dealing with the redemption of land (Lev. 25.26), a slave (Lev. 25.51), the firstborn (Num. 18.15) and the like, they tend to forget the far more central and theologically significant occurrence of the word in Deutero-Isaiah where it is closely associated with the archetype of God's saving act in the Exodus (see Is. 14.14 ff.; 49.7 ff., etc.).[10] The first Christian theologians who were seized of this profound intuition of the unity of sacred history saw the death-resurrection of the Lord as a new and final exodus, but they saw it largely through the projection of the Egyptian exodus in the writings of the anonymous prophet of the exile. It is not just a question of the title of Servant or of the literary use of this passion-figure in the gospel passion-narrative. There is, besides, a whole framework of reference for what we find in the New Testament on the redemptive mission of Christ. A quick check will reveal that there are far more direct or in-direct references in the New Testament to Isaiah 40–55 than to any other part of the Old Testament – giving a fair idea of the theo-logical significance of this book.

Another and related point, often overlooked, is the idea of solidarity and corporate personality involved in the idea of a *go'el* as meaning in the first place "kinsman", "blood-avenger". This would open up social implications of the redemption richly developed in the East but rather lost sight of in the West once the idea of penal substitution (and a host of subsidiary influences) took over.

A digression suggests itself here on the interaction between liturgy, theology and popular piety. The concentration of popular piety in the late Middle Ages on the suffering humanity of the Redeemer (*via crucis,* feast of the *Mater dolorosa,* liturgical com-positions of Jacopone da Todi)[11] accompanied the gradual

[10] See my article in *Concilium,* December 1966, pp. 22–26 (American edn., Vol. 20, 41–50).

[11] This process is described and illustrated in A. G. Hebert, *Liturgy and Society,* London, 1935 (Faber edition, 112–38). It is important to note that this late medieval pietism is continued in that of the Lutherans as could be seen by comparing da Todi with Paul Gerhardt. Luther himself was brought up in the same tradition of spiritua-lity which produced *The Imitation of Christ.*

etiolation of the biblical and patristic synthesis on the Redemption. Thus it is no surprise that we express our sympathy with the suffering Lord and our gratitude that he has taken our place on the scaffold, *iustus pro iniustis,* in terms of a theology of penal substitution which is still quite influential:

> Thou for us the path hast trod
> Of the dreadful wrath of God,
> Thou the cup of fire hast drained
> Till its light alone remained. . . .

The contrast with the emphasis is the well-known composition of Newman (from *The Dream of Gerontius*), coming as it does from a man formed directly on a biblical and patristic, not scholastic, theology, is very instructive:

> O wisest love, that flesh and blood
> Which did in Adam fail
> Should strive afresh against the foe,
> Should strive and should prevail!

Here is implied: that in Christ the whole of humanity suffers and triumphs since he is our blood-brother; that the one redemptive act envisages redemption and new life, new humanity through death; that Jesus is delivered up to death and put on the cross through the love not the anger of the Father.

One final point that ought to be mentioned here with regard to the Redemption is the absence of any treatment of cosmic redemption dealt with so movingly in Romans 8. It is true that the renewal of the cosmos is dealt with in *de Novissimis,* if very briefly, but its absence here involves a loss of proportion and it fits very awkwardly into a scheme which is already very individualistic in approach.

This leads on naturally to a second example which illustrates the same kind of difficulty in method and approach, namely, eschatology. It would seem natural to close the theological synthesis with a treatise *de Deo consummatore* dealing with the orientation of existence in the eschatological aeon of the Church, indwelt by the risen Lord whose very presence is *pignus futurae gloriae.* In the textbooks, however, the consummation of the

Church is considered in a brief scholion to what happens to the physical world.[12] It is likewise significant that St Thomas has to consign this question, in the Supplement to the third part of the *Summa,* to "the things which belong to the resurrection", the final resurrection, understood. No doubt the basic difficulty here is to know how to integrate the *eschaton* of the individual Christian into that of the redeemed community and the cosmos, and thus avoid falling into an individualistic approach – a danger which has beset Roman Catholic theology at every level. There is also the problem of time and the enormous change in our attitude to nature and the time–space environment. This challenge is hardly taken up at all and is only beginning to be taken seriously in theological thinking about "the last things". This would involve giving more attention to the question of cosmic redemption, the destiny of mankind seen in an evolutionary light, and less to questions such as whether it is "convenient" that there should be plants and animals in "the new earth" – rather in the line of St Thomas's lucubrations on the hair and finger-nails of the risen body.[13] There is throughout a marked disinclination to incorporate into the synthesis the advances made in our understanding of nature and man as a historical being.

This question of the understanding of time is basic. What happens to the Jewish apocalyptic concept of the two ages, the semantic tension between "age" and "world"? What of the tension implied in ecclesial existence between the "already" and the "not yet"? This is surely the kind of question to which theological thinking on the Scriptures might be expected to provide an answer. And then in the detailed exposition of relevant texts there is need of discrimination and critical awareness. The textbook approach usually demanded a definite location for hell – one even suggests that it is probably to be situated in "the lower parts of the earth", whatever that means.[14] That hell is a place is

---

[12] See the B.A.C. *Summa,* IV, 1061, and A. Piolanti, *De Novissimis,* Rome 1949,[3] 169–70.

[13] *Ibid.,* 1061; *Summa,* Suppl. 3a, qu. 80, art. 2.

[14] B.A.C. *Summa,* 991, thus accepting the cosmology of Dante as against that of Milton who, in taking the whole universe as his scenario, reflects the advance in understanding made in the intervening four centuries.

defended by appeal to Luke 16.28 and Acts 1.24, neglecting the fact that the former is a story (the Rich Man and Lazarus) and that "to go to one's place" in the latter reflects an Aramaic euphemism for "to die". The presentation of a world-end as a judgment by fire comes to us in mythological terms as used commonly by Jewish apocalyptic writers. Fire throughout the Scriptures is a polyvalent symbol or image: judgment within history symbolized by the fire of a burning city, the track of a victorious army, lightning, thunderbolt, volcanic eruptions, etc. Jesus, too, used this kind of language, and in more than one case we have close parallels from contemporary or near-contemporary writing for the way he speaks. So, for example, the judgment scene with the Son of Man sitting on his glorious throne (Mt. 25.31 ff.) occurs in the Similitudes of Enoch. All this has to be taken carefully into account before passing on to making theological generalizations.

This is particularly true of the cosmic eschaton. The basic scriptural figure of the final world-catastrophe is of a dissolution into an amorphous, primary state, a *tohu wabohu,* Chaos-come-again. As long as the cosmic *materia prima* or world-stuff was thought to be water the end of such a world could come about only by means of a reduction to the watery chaos from which it arose. This will emerge clearly from a reading of the Genesis Flood story comparing it with the Creation prologue in Genesis 1. In the first century A.D. the basic world-stuff was represented as fire, both in philosophical thinking (the Stoics) and in Jewish apocalyptic imagery. This explains the contrast in the Petrine epistles (1 Pet. 3.20; 2 Pet. 2.5 ff.) between the "old world" before the Flood which came to a watery end and the present world destined to return to its primary element which is fire (2 Pet. 3.5–7). To establish this does not of course render theological speculation on this subject superfluous; on the contrary, the theologian's task begins here where the exegete's ends. The one cannot by-pass the other.

There are other points of particular interpretation on this subject which we can only mention, such as the exact meaning of terms like "tartarus" and "Hades" borrowed from mythology, the use made of descriptive figures such as "the worm which does not die and the fire which is not put out" (Mk 9.48, cf.

Is. 66.24 and Jg. 16.17), how the biblical writers thought of the *parousia* – essentially a political metaphor – and so on.

Other examples could be given of divergence in attitude and method between dogmatic theology of the pre-conciliar kind and biblical theology. There is, for example, the treatise on the Kingship of Christ (summarized in Pius X's encyclical) which starts out from the definition of monarchy at one stage of European civilization (the medieval concept of *regnum* in particular). The biblical idea of kingship and kingdom was elaborated in an entirely different milieu and does not necessarily admit of the theological conclusions drawn from the "received" elaboration. There is the concept of sacrifice and priesthood with the dangerous tendency to extrapolate back into the Old Testament. There is the treatise on Grace, ontologized and dehistoricized, overshadowed by the historical legacy of the *de auxiliis* controversy with its now incomprehensible vocabulary. True, we are now much more aware of the inadequacies of the older method; but we are as yet far from being in a position to draw up a new systematic theology based on the new (or, better, recovered) insights.

There is certainly a lesson here for both exegete and dogmatic theologian: for the former, the need to be constantly aware of the theological implications of his work. He has to make his way between the Scylla of a purely philological and semantic discipline and the Charybdis of an autonomous, take-it-or-leave-it biblical theology. It is not enough for him simply to explain the Bible in terms of the culture in which it came into existence since people cannot be expected to follow Pius XI's advice and become "spiritual Semites". For the latter, there is the need to throw off the last vestiges of the defensive and apologetic approach characteristic of the Counter-Reformation period, perhaps to abandon altogether the *argumentum ex sacra scriptura* and remodel theological presentation accordingly. We do not as yet see how this will work out in practice; but we may hope for a reformulation in the not too distant future which will reflect our increased understanding of the relation of Scripture and Tradition by taking the dialogue between the Word and the Church as the starting-point of theological reflection. This will not be just the outcome of an itch for reform at any cost – quite the contrary – or a vague and unformulated discontent, but of the desire to give to theology a decisively pastoral orientation in this age of lay participation and ecumenical hope.

II

Rethinking Revelation

THE RECEIVED TEACHING on revelation before the Council, as presented in the manuals in use in seminaries and thence percolating down to the consciousness of Catholics by means of religious instruction, was that God has revealed certain propositions or truths the acceptance of which was necessary for salvation. Theologians thought it legitimate to define the minimum number of such truths to be assented to in order to reach this end, such as, that God exists, that he is good, that he rewards the good and punishes the evil. As Bishop Butler put it,[1] revelation was thought of rather as a third-personal enrichment of the intellect than a second-personal dialogue. This way of thinking was so much taken for granted in the last century that Vatican I's statement on the subject (issued on 24 March 1870) said nothing at all on the nature of revelation but began at once with the possibility of knowing God by reason, passing on to speak of the sources of supernatural revelation "in written books and traditions which did not find their way into writing". This view was still widely held among the participants of Vatican II, at least in the early stages. Moreover, the standard view of Christ was that he was the emissary of God, a messenger bringing divine teaching to men. His miracles, including the Resurrection considered as the climax of the miracles, were signs confirming his status as divinely-sent messenger and consequently the genuineness of the teachings which he communicated.

This view of revelation issues in a clear picture of the Christian life. To be a Christian is first of all to accept certain propositions and the moral standards which they entail. Christianity, therefore, tends to be identified with orthodoxy, the ability to give correct

[1] In *The Theology of Vatican II,* Darton, Longman and Todd, London, 1967.

16

answers to certain specific questions. The tendency to think of revelation as giving us additional *objects* of knowledge ("truths") over and above those which we possess already results in a distinction or dichotomy between ordinary knowledge and experience and the knowledge and experience which are specifically religious. It implies, therefore, a distinct category of *religious* knowledge and experience. I want to try to show in what follows how and to what extent this dichotomy is being overcome in recent thinking about biblical revelation, and how, in the light of this, the constitution *Dei Verbum* of Vatican II may be assessed.

*   *   *

In the Bible God is everywhere represented as speaking and acting. He speaks when he creates the world, he talks to the man and woman in Eden, the prophets usually preface their utterances with the formula "thus says (or, has said) Yahweh", he speaks in these last days through the Son. He makes the world, he makes man, we find him walking in the garden and through the Israelite camp, he even rides in the wind and marches in the juniper trees. He leads Israel out of Egypt, makes a covenant, he is often angry, passionate or jealous. Now all these are very odd ways of talking about God, and in so far as they are general statements about him, unrelated to ordinary human experience, starting from "the other end", we should have no hesitation in characterizing them as mythical.[2] And yet, since we are dealing with God speaking and acting, how can we start anywhere else but at "the other end"?

Let us, at any rate, try to begin at *our end*, with the way in which the word *revelation* is commonly used. We say, for example, "that was a revelation to me" when someone we know, a friend, acts in a way for us totally unexpected. All of a sudden we get

[2] According to Bultmann, any general statements about God which are unrelated to historical existence in some way are mythological. The only non-mythological way of speaking of God is in terms of personal existence. See chapter 5 of his *Jesus Christ and Mythology*, Charles Scribner's Sons, New York, 1958; S.C.M. Press, London, 1960.

an insight into his character or situation which can in its turn even give us a new insight into human character in general or our own situation. We have what Bishop Ramsey likes to call a disclosure. A biblical example, chosen at random, might be the infidelity of Hosea's wife. Let us suppose, for the moment, that this was an event which really happened as described (there is no reason why we should not). The experience of marital infidelity is not in itself either extraordinary or of rare occurrence. But it opened up for Hosea a new way of looking at the relations between God and the community to which he belonged, a community which believed itself to have a special relationship to God. It did not provide him with new objects of knowledge, but it enabled him to know what he already knew in a different way and at a deeper level. It was, literally, a revelation to him.

There is a possible source of confusion in giving biblical examples of revelations or disclosures in that many of the media of such revelations are not part of common human experience in anything like the way that marital infidelity is. Some are clearly of an extraordinary nature, such as the experience – however we explain it – which Isaiah had in the temple, others ambiguously so, such as visions of a plumb-line or a basket of ripe fruit which could be traced back to the everyday experience of those who had the experience in question. In antiquity, if it did not rain when expected to or the goats failed to give milk, the revelation of the cause of the failure was sought, not as would be the case today, from a meteorologist or vetinerary surgeon respectively, but from a medicine man or the local *guru* or even in the stars or the entrails of a disembowelled animal. This, of course, is not the kind of revelation we are talking about here, but it is worth mentioning at this point since we find that extraordinary media of revelation such as urim and thummim (involving the use of something equivalent to dice), the ephod, ecstatic prophets and the like are progressively left behind, leaving the way open for revelation arising out of what is central and even ordinary in human experience.

The break-up of Hosea's marriage was the starting-point of a revelation for Hosea personally. It became a revelation, vicariously but no less really, for those of his countrymen who listened to his preaching and later read the book which bears his name. The appropriation at second remove of the experience is reflected, among other things, in the editorial history of the book. It is difficult to see how any kind of revelation can be anything but personal in origin, despite the insistence in so much recent writing on the social aspects of biblical revelation and inspiration. The Exodus is generally taken to be the starting-point of the whole revelational process. It is so presented in the Bible and described, in the Old Testament, in the exalted language of saga, heroic recital and even myth.[3] But a knowledge of the history of the Near East in the century or so after the Amarna age reveals that a population movement of this kind, involving renunciation of allegiance to a monarch and a journey in search of a settled residence in the sown land, was not such an extraordinary event. In Amos 9.7 God declares that the same kind of thing had happened to the Philistines and the Syrians as happened to the Israelites. If the Egyptians had left behind a bulletin recording the event, we may be sure it would have read rather differently from the account in the Book of Exodus. Only some Israelite (Moses?) came to see in this something new and unique, and communicated this insight to the others. This insight into a social or political event, not *in itself* unique or extraordinary, is unpacked in different ways throughout the Old Testament and dynamically reinterpreted in the New. It achieves the status of a political and religious symbol – the passage from slavery to freedom – and thus becomes a means of further insight or disclosure in its own right. From being a *personal* insight it becomes *social*. But it is first personal.

If all that the biblical writers had wanted to do was to record one of several population-movements in the thirteenth century B.C. they would have said simply that Israel came out of Egypt. In saying, as they do, that God *led* Israel out of Egypt they are not committing themselves in the first place to a statement about God acting – in the same category as, for example, God eating, talking or walking. This would be pure mythology. They are expressing

---

[3] The last most clearly in Is. 51.9–10.

the revelational character of the event as perceived in Israel and opening up its possibilities for the future. There is no God-in-himself but only a God-for-Israel, seen in the recurring divine self-predication: "I am the Lord *your* God who brought you out of the land of Egypt, out of the house of bondage."

A mistake to which Roman Catholics, perhaps more than most others, have been prone is that of thinking that the revelational character of events can be positively verified either on the grounds that biblical language is in some way incorrigible (fundamentalism) or that the event in question can be shown to be unique. *All* historical events are unique in so far as non-recurrent, but that is a different matter. We have just seen that the Exodus is not unique in the sense of non-typical. There was more than one exodus. We could take another example from the account of creation in the first chapter of the Bible. No one outside of the lunatic fringe now supposes that this is meant to be a revelation of new knowledge about how the world began, arranged neatly in chronological order. To think of God acting in this way is just as mythological, if less crudely so, as other cosmogonies which speak of the world originating out of the copulation of divine beings or the cutting up of a defeated monster or the self-procured seed of a god. The revelational character of this chapter consists in the attempt to make us see the world in a certain way. The author (in the singular) has had an insight which has imposed order on and given meaning to the *tohu wabohu,* the chaos of disparate sense-impressions which go to make up his – and our – life in the world. He is trying to make us share this insight by thinking of the world in a certain way, even in a certain order, with special reference to the movement of the mind from the vast impersonal entities and forces in the world to the personal, the centre of perception – "*let us make* man in our image, after our likeness".[4] This too, we repeat, is a personal insight or disclosure, though of course it is the insight of a person living in a certain society and community and sharing in a liturgical life with others. The relevance of this last can be seen in that Psalm 136 also moves,

---

[4] This is worked out in a very illuminating way in chapter 4 of I. T. Ramsey, *Religion and Science: Conflict and Synthesis,* S.P.C.K. London, 1964.

in its praise of creation, from the impersonal to the personal –
God praised in the creation, God praised in the historical
experience of Israel.

The difference between the old and the new way of looking at
revelation is often expressed as the difference between a propo-
sitional and a historical view of revelation. In so far as Judaism
and Christianity, regarded as religions, are not based on general
propositions or religious truths in the way that might be considered
true of, say, Taoism or Buddhism, this description would have
some value. But of course the Scriptures also contain propositions
of different kinds. We find definitions such as "faith is the assurance of things hoped for" (in Heb. 11.1), general statements of
a religious nature such as "in the beginning God created the
heavens and the earth" (Gen. 1.1 – if this is the correct parsing),
moral imperatives such as "observe the sabbath day to keep it
holy" (Deut. 5.12). These, too, are just as much objects of
revelation as events such as the Exodus. The mistake easily made
with these, however, is to put them into a separate category and
treat them as different, as if the language in which they come to us
were in some way incorrigible, containing and exhausting the
reality towards which the words direct our attention. General
statements of this kind, even irreducible dogmas – whether
coming to us in scriptural language or that of councils and popes –
have the same function as the description of events, to direct
our attention to the root-perception from which they spring, in
the hope that we may come to share this insight and appropriate
it for ourselves. This may be why doctrinal creeds issuing from
councils used to be known as *symbols of faith*. Not to recognize
this is to run the risk of falling into an idolatrous worship of
words, either biblical or otherwise.

It still remains true, however, that biblical revelation is in a
special way tied up with history. It is claimed for this particular
segment of history that it is capable of revealing a real progress
and, in the progress, a pattern. This does not imply that we
scrutinize it in order to see general religious truths emerging.
In Psalm 136, referred to above, God is praised serially as: he
who smote the first-born of Egypt, who brought Israel out from

among them, who divided the Red Sea, who overthrew Pharaoh and his hosts in it, who led his people through the wilderness, eventually giving them the land as an inheritance. Here we have a progressive disclosure through a series of what the same psalm calls God's "great wonders". Whether extraordinary events such as the first and third of the series happened as described in the Old Testament, that is, whether they were miraculous, is a subject which can be discussed. It need not detain us at this point since a miracle, to be what it is claimed to be, has to be *perceived* as such and therefore requires a subjective commitment in advance which in its turn depends on a perception of what the event or events mean as a whole. Once this perception is born, the events are seen to reveal God present as a saving reality. It is only then that they can make a total demand on the one perceiving, that through them God can address him.

It is common practice to emphasize the peculiarity of biblical revelation by contrasting it with Greek religious thought on this subject. This is all the more apposite in that, right from the beginning, the doctrine of revelation has been elaborated by people (the "Fathers of the Church") trained in Greek philosophy. Greek thought in general presupposes an eternal world alongside the historical world in which we live. The latter is intelligible only in so far as it embodies a principle which must be sought beyond it – whether the *nous* of Anaxagoras or the *idea* of Plato or the *logos* of the Stoics. The historical world is capable of revealing to the perceptive and wise man the eternal and unchanging reality beyond. What *is* is revealed behind and through what *seems to be*. For the Bible on the other hand "the essential thing . . . is not to be found in what always is, but in what happens".[5] Hence the deep involvement in the political and sociological factors of existence which comes through at every stage, most particularly in the Prophets. And since revelation is still going on, mediated through Christ to the Church living in the historical world, "the Church must take seriously her continuing life in world history so as to understand what God is asking of her at

---

[5] A. Oepke, Art. *apokalyptō*, G. Kittel, *Theological Dictionary of the New Testament*, Grand Rapids, 1965, III, 572.

each moment".[6] There is something here very different from the seminary textbook idea of revelation.

Perhaps the most important advance in our understanding of revelation is that we have come to realize that it must be characterized by dialogue. This is already implied in the term *Word of God*, the traditional paraphrase, since *word* necessarily implies the one to whom the word is addressed, a person capable of reception and response. It is therefore possible to speak of the *Word of God* only in an interpersonal situation. Even if we start "at the other end" and use an expression such as "God speaks" we must imply a human activity or reactivity of some kind. In this assumed context, for God to speak must mean not that he expresses *something* but that he expresses himself, and for God to express himself means to give himself, implying "a self-offering for friendship".[7] This, however, is meaningless unless we think at the same time of the perception, reception and commitment of those to whom the offer is addressed. The Bible therefore cannot *contain* revelation, if we understand this latter as the original impulse from God. It records the reaction or response elicited by a "word" which had already been spoken. It points to that "word" but does not encompass it. Biblical history, therefore, will not be of the neutral, objective kind (though no history is really of that kind). It will be (and it is) both epiphanous, revealing a hidden presence or "word", and a public confession of failure to respond in faith to that presence or to take up the challenge of a demanding dialogue. A prophetic book records the response of some person specially sensitive to the deeper significance of the events, but this response, as it is communicated to others either directly or indirectly, is, so to speak, built into the revelational process, making it possible for God to continue speaking. It is a dialogue of the kind which must end either in ultimate union or estrangement.

A final and decisive test of this dialogue-character of revelation is the biblical Christ in whom, as Christians believe, is the final self-revelation of God and the only full human response. In him

[6] G. Moran, *Theology of Revelation*, Herder and Herder, 1966, 21.
[7] Oepke, *op. cit.*, 591.

God has said everything which he will ever say. He is the Word fully incorporated into history, that is, made flesh. In him humanity says its Yes to that revealing word – "in him it is always Yes" (2 Cor. 1.19). Through him God continues to reveal himself in the form of new truth, and so the dialogue continues. Implied in this is the need not to absolutize the Scriptures since they witness to a development in the revelational process the end of which has not yet been reached. They are unique and regulative of the Church's life because of their privileged witness to the final Word spoken in Christ, but it is only a personal existence lived fully in the world which can draw out the meaning of the Christ-event and so make it possible for the dialogue to continue its course.

*　　　*　　　*

If we are not to absolutize scriptural statements, this will be true *a fortiori* for those of ecclesiastical authority. In no document more than in *Dei Verbum* is the human element in evidence. As is well known, a first draft was presented to the Council in the first session and promptly thrown out as inadequate. A second draft was prepared by an *ad hoc* committee and went beyond the first in not simply equating revelation with revealed teaching. It also deleted the first chapter of the first draft entitled "The Two Sources of Revelation" and substituted for it two chapters, the first on the nature of revelation, the second on its transmission. This in its turn was subjected to much revision in and after the third session, the final document being promulgated in November 1965, three years after the rejection of the first draft.

There can be no doubt at all that this document represents an advance on the nineteenth-century idea of revelation. It states at once that God reveals himself "through deeds and words", thereby getting away from the restrictive idea that revelation is concerned with the communication of divine teaching and nothing else. It implies that revelation is primarily through historical events or personal historical experience; that we do not have to extract "truths" from the history but that the meaning is somehow *in* the history or experience. Thus history can be seen as containing insight-situations in the way referred to above.

Even more important, perhaps, *Dei Verbum* goes some way to overcoming the post-Reformation emphasis on faith as primarily assent to propositions or, at a less theological level, as the ability and willingness to give orthodox answers to certain specified questions. Faith is first of all a life-commitment, coming off the fence of a neutral existence. Any revelation gives some kind of discernment, but it is the nature of the Christian revelation to imply not just discernment but a life-commitment. This is the real meaning of Paul's phrase about "the obedience of faith" quoted in the first chapter of the document.

There is also a great advance on previous official statements in the recognition that the ultimate source of the disclosure-discernment-commitment process lies *beyond* the words of Scripture, beyond the continuing life of the Church in the world, being something to which these point but with which they cannot be identified. It is stated that tradition includes all that makes up the life in faith of the Christian community growing and expanding from one age to the next. What is passed on is not a clearly defined body of doctrine – like some kind of family heirloom – but the life of the Church itself, *omne quod ipsa est* (par. 8). Revelation, therefore, cannot be confined to a book. However we define it, it is something that takes place in real human experience and is then communicated either orally or in writing – there is no essential difference.

Thus far, therefore, we have a real advance full of positive ecumenical significance. But it is precisely here, in the attempt to define Tradition and Scripture, that we come up against the main difficulty. There is some confusion, to begin with, in the use of terms. In chapter 2, *The Transmission of Divine Revelation,* it is stated that there is only one source of revelation, God's self-disclosure in Christ, so it is a question of the means by which this is communicated. Here there is some confusion. "The Word of God" is used of both the Scriptures and Tradition (par. 10) and "traditions" are said to be passed on orally and in writing (par. 8). Elsewhere in the same chapter tradition is defined so as to exclude

C

Scripture. Par. 8 refers to the apostolic preaching expressed "in a special way" in the inspired books, and there is the last-minute addition of Paul VI in par. 9 rejecting the *Scriptura sola* idea and in doing so at this point inevitably blurring the effect of the statements made at the beginning of the chapter on the unity of the revelational process. "Tradition" is also used of the *diadoche* or apostolic succession, or so it would appear from the context.[8]

This confusion in the use of terms which reflects divided opinion on the Council floor – and no doubt also the misgivings of Paul VI himself – leaves some questions of the highest ecumenical importance up in the air. Perhaps the time was not ripe for discussing them, but discuss them we must if we are to make any further progress. What are these "traditions" (par. 8) which have been passed on orally and are not contained in the Scriptures? Can any of them be identified as doctrines currently accepted in Roman Catholicism, doctrines such as the Immaculate Conception and the Assumption of Mary? Again, what sort of control does Scripture exercise upon the life of the Church and the magisterium in particular, granted that, as the document allows, the teaching office is the servant of the Word of God (par. 10)? Are there developments within the Church which can be defined as unscriptural and which consequently can be considered as reversible? Despite the advance in the basic understanding of revelation, reflected partially in this document, there will be little further progress until these questions are honestly answered.

[8] "In order to keep the gospel forever whole and alive within the Church, the apostles left bishops as their successors, handing over their own teaching role to them. This sacred tradition, *therefore,* and sacred Scripture of both the Old and the New Testament are like a mirror in which the pilgrim Church on earth looks at God . . " – towards the end of par. 7 of chapter II. From the translation of W. M. Abbott and J. Gallagher, Chapman, London, 1966, 115.

III

Rethinking Biblical Inspiration

USED OF THE SCRIPTURES, inspiration is a metaphor which may
have something in its favour but can be rather misleading. It
tends to give the idea that the Scriptures contain a series of
oracular utterances and, whatever else we may say, oracular
exegesis is *out*. But even if we accept what we find in the Bible as
literary composition obeying stylistic laws which must be put in
the context of a past culture, the term hardly fits. Some passages,
in fact, look distinctly uninspired. The Harvard scholar Pfeiffer
spoke of 2 Samuel 7 (Nathan's prophetic address to David) as
"a wretched and inept piece of writing" while another American
scholar characterized it as "monkish drivel", though it is a little
difficult to see why they picked on that passage rather than some
others one can think of. There is also another source of misunderstanding. Much of the "heroic" matter in Judges and elsewhere
was produced originally, in all probability, by schools of
rhapsodists and only later worked up into prose form, eventually
finding its way into the canonical books. According to the
accepted terminology, the poetical originals would be uninspired
while the canonical prose narratives, further removed from the
creative centre, would be inspired. A question of words, perhaps,
but providing, one suspects, a barrier against understanding
and penetration.

The term "inspiration" goes back to the Vulgate (and, before
that, the Old Latin) translation of a phrase in 2 Timothy 3.16
which the R.S.V. englishes as: "All scripture is inspired by God" –
referring of course to what we now call the Old Testament and
possibly also to some Christian writings already being read in the
assemblies. Not all Church writers understood the term in the
same way and it did not gain general currency until the sixteenth

century. It was not even used at the Council of Trent and therefore can hardly be taken as the only or even the principal way of expressing what the Church has thought throughout the ages of the unique authority of her sacred writings. More frequently this has been expressed by speaking of God as the author of the Scriptures, implying that God, so to speak, takes full responsibility for what is written, using a human author as instrument. This way of speaking has been "canonized" by the official pronouncements of the magisterium, conciliar and otherwise.

When, however, we come to look at it more closely, this idea of dual authorship is very difficult to visualize. On the one hand, it could easily lead us to the idea of God dictating what he wants written to an amanuensis who does his job mechanically, rather like an automaton, in which case the Scriptures are reduced to a form of automatic writing. On the other, we might think of God commissioning a ghost-writer who then goes on to work up the idea or story into presentable and intelligible form. Both alternatives have been defended in different periods of the Church's history, yet both are clearly inadequate.

This problem of the two authors is the first of several involved in rethinking biblical inspiration which Rahner discusses in his small treatise on this subject.[1] He concludes that if we wish to keep this way of speaking and at the same time leave the human writer (Ezekiel or Paul or anon.) as author in the real sense of the word, we must think of God as author in a way different from that in which we have thought heretofore. Rahner suggests that God is the author of the Scriptures only in so far as he is author, that is, originator, of the Church. He is the author of the Scriptures because in willing the Church to be what he wanted it to be he also had to will the Scriptures as a constituent element in the Church's foundation. When we speak of God as author, we are speaking of his causality with regard to the Bible, but this, Rahner insists, must be seen within his causality with regard to the Church, and in particular the apostolic Church as the norm

---

[1] *Inspiration in the Bible,* Herder & Herder, 1961. The unwary ought to be warned that there are many errors of translation in the English version, beginning with the title.

for all future time. To say this does not, of course, solve all the problems and may even raise some new ones. One example would be the inspiration of the Old Testament with relation to God's predetermination of the apostolic Church. This Rahner goes on to discuss while other problems he leaves to us. The point is that we are drawn away from an individualistic and mechanistic way of viewing the question and on to a new line of thought which begins with the community as a whole.

This becomes clearer when Rahner goes on, a little later, to ask another question: how does the Church know that the Scriptures are inspired? The classical Lutheran theory started out from that *gustus internus* which the Christian experienced, or was supposed to experience, in reading the Scriptures. There is something here, as indeed there must be in an experiential approach of this kind, but we are left asking what happens to a scripture such as Paul's letter (more like a postcard) to Philemon which can hardly be expected to produce such a result. If we take the easy way out and posit a revelation left behind from the apostolic age, we then have the task of explaining why the Church took so long – several centuries – to make up her mind which writings were inspired and which were not. Here again, the strength of Rahner's approach lies in the fact that he starts out from our own experience of what the Church is: *the Church, filled with the Holy Spirit, recognizes something as connatural with her own being in the writings which have come down from the apostolic age,* but her appropriation of the Scriptures is part of the assimilation and realization of her own identity which is worked out slowly within the historical process, and therefore takes time.

He also seeks for an answer to the question how we can speak meaningfully of an inspiration of which the writer is unconscious – a possibility taken for granted in the terms of reference within which the early Church writers and medieval scholastics worked. The writer, he says in effect, may well be, and usually will be, unconscious of some miraculous movement within himself the source of which, however, he traces to an outside agency. What he *is* conscious of is that he belongs to a particular community and that he communicates not as an individual but as a member of this community in which he knows that God is progressively revealing his ultimate purpose. What therefore we call inspiration is really a function of the existence of the one, holy community, *in fieri* in Old Testament times, *in esse* in the apostolic Church.

This question of an inspiration granted to someone unconscious of it leads on to a further point. St Thomas covers this possibility in the abstract by distinguishing between what he calls the *acceptio rei* and the *iudicium de re accepta*. These are, respectively, the manifold ways in which the psyche is enriched with knowledge, ideas, experience, *including revealed truths,* and the judgment which subjects this received material to scrutiny. Applying this to biblical inspiration, it means that the writer may use sources, collect his material, conjure up ideas and images in a purely human way but that what is in fact communicated is the result of a judgment elicited by means of a divine enlightenment of the faculties. This seems to leave the way open for the full co-operation of the human author as instrument while retaining the essential point of God as the real, ultimate author of what is written.

While being satisfactory in the abstract, this explanation is really too conceptual. It appears to embody a procedure only too common in the scholastic tradition – you have a difficulty and, in order to overcome it, you invent a terminology in which it can be stated and make that do for a solution. Thus, when we read certain scriptural passages, we are led to ask how an inspiration of which the writer is evidently unconscious can have any real effect. A classical example is Luke's Prologue. One less known is the Second Book of Maccabees, canonical only for Roman Catholic Christians. The writer tells us that his work is a résumé of the *History* of a certain Jason of Cyrene. He added nothing to what he found in his source and the work of summarizing was tough going. He says at the end:

If the writing of it is good and has succeeded that is what I desired. But if it is not so perfect and is no more than mediocre it must be pardoned me. For just as it is hurtful to drink either always wine or always water, but pleasant to use sometimes the one and sometimes the other, so if the speech is always nicely framed it will not be gratifying to the reader. But here it shall be ended.

– and not a moment too soon, we feel inclined to add. Would it not be more reasonable to interpret the author's or compiler's "inspiration" to write as coming to him in the first place from his community-consciousness by means of which, in each particular case, God guides and builds up his people?

The drawback inherent in this received terminology is, therefore, that it can lead us to think of the biblical writer as a medium or an automaton or at least as an individual, isolated recipient of a grace or charism unrelated to the society of which he is a part and without which he would never have written. There is also another drawback, that it starts out from the relatively modern idea of authorship and book-production. Moses is the author of a work called *The Pentateuch* in the same way, more or less, as Darwin is the author of *The Origin of Species*. This could be maintained at a time when the Bible was understood as a collection of separate books each one by a well-known author: the Pentateuch by Moses, Psalms by David, Proverbs, the Canticle, Wisdom and Qoheleth by Solomon, the sixty-six chapters of Isaiah by the eighth-century prophet of that name, Malachi by Malachi, etc. This, however, is no longer possible. The Pentateuch in its final form is the outcome of a long process of oral and written traditioning. It is essentially a sedimentarization of tradition, a precipitate of the faith of a believing community throughout many centuries. Many of the psalms have a long history and were used, with changes, adaptations and modifications of various kinds, in public liturgy. Books like Hosea and Isaiah are, in their final form, compilations made by groups of disciples who had gathered round a distinguished prophetic figure and thus formed a "school". We have therefore to allow for anonymity and collective authorship, sometimes extending over a very long period.

Reflection along these lines has led other scholars to conclusions similar to those of Rahner in recent years. Among these we might mention in particular a short study of John McKenzie which emphasizes the social aspects of this doctrine.[2] There is no space here even to summarize his argument, but an example (not from McKenzie) will illustrate the major point at issue. The Book of Deuteronomy, it is clear, went through several "editions" before reaching its final form. The heterogeneous body of laws which make up the central part of the book (12–26) went through a long period of adaptation in response to changing conditions and is clearly older than the framework in which we now find it. It is just as clear that, for example, the law about kings could not come from the time of Moses as it is that the law imposing a speed limit of 70 m.p.h. could not have risen in eighteenth-century England. The homiletic material of which the book is full was developed in levitical "schools" and traditioned for a considerable period before reaching its final form, so that it is really the levitical preacher and not Moses who is speaking. The same for the liturgical material contained in this book; it is not really the original group at Sinai which is being addressed but the congregation of a later day, "you, all of you who are alive this day". Who then is inspired here? We cannot restrict inspiration to the last "editor" who gave the whole book its final form, presuming, that is, that there was only one. How far back, then, have we to push inspiration? Will it cover also the period of oral tradition? Does it apply to all who, even in the slightest degree, were responsible for the traditioning?

It is at this stage that we begin to wonder whether the individualistic approach to inspiration is not beginning to break down. The alternative, McKenzie suggests, is to relate the individual oral composer, traditioner or writer to the society in which he lives and in which alone his action is significant. This means that although individuals will always be the recipients of an impulse which has its origin in God, its medium or vehicle must be the community, either directly or indirectly. This gives a new significance to the Scriptures, both Old and New Testaments, as the expression of a particular and unique social consciousness.

All recent attempts to rethink biblical inspiration have moved

[2] "Social Character of Inspiration", *Catholic Biblical Quarterly*, 24 (1962), 115–24.

towards a greater appreciation of its social aspect.[3] This is true even of the more theologically elaborated exposition of Benoit[4] since, in categorizing inspiration as a charism, he implies at least that it is orientated towards the whole community. The charismatic gifts, according to Paul, are exercised in the community and exist "so that the Church may be built up" (1 Cor. 14.5). He is, however, less concerned than the writers just mentioned with an explanation of the relations and interactions between individual and society and more with the psychological processes involved. He is also concerned to show how closely inspiration is related to revelation. The charism of revelation refers to all acts of speculative knowledge elicited under divine impulse, that of inspiration to all the activity involved in communicating this knowledge. One wonders, however, whether this goes far enough towards relating these terms to the concrete historical existence of the community. One wonders whether revelation and inspiration could not be considered as conceptually distinct aspects of the one providence by which the people is guided throughout its history into the fullness of community in which the final salvation offered through Christ is to be effected.

It is this development within revelation recorded in the Scriptures and guided by the Holy Spirit which we too often tend to overlook. It is also the same Spirit who is present within the continued search of the Christian community since the end of the apostolic age to understand what has been entrusted to it and in so doing to rediscover continually its own identity.

[3] See especially D. J. McCarthy, "Personality, Society and Inspiration," *Theological Studies*, 24 (1963), 553–76.

[4] P. Benoit, *Inspiration and the Bible*, Sheed & Ward, London, 1965.

VI

Rethinking Biblical Inerrancy

IN CATHOLIC TEACHING biblical inerrancy (biblical truth would be surely a better term) has been understood to mean: (1) that the Scriptures are in fact free from any error, and (2) that it is antecedently impossible for any error to be found in them. The difficulty has then been to know from which proposition to begin. One could begin from the second, establish it to one's satisfaction, and thus dispense conveniently with the need for taking account of actual cases in the Scriptures which might cause some embarrassment. This, however, is the way of fundamentalism. If, to take the hoariest example possible, it is recorded that the "big fish" swallowed Jonah this must be true. If, however, the Scriptures had recorded the reverse we should have accepted that with the same equanimity. For this approach there are, on principle, no problems.

If, instead, we start with the first proposition and go on to point out, as we must, that there are many affirmations in the Scriptures which are clearly erroneous we find ourselves obliged to look again at the use of the word *inerrant*. Errors in history are the most obvious since the most open to verification. Thus we read in Judith 1.2 that Nebuchadnezzar was king of the Assyrians, which he was not, in Tobit 1.15 that Sennacherib was son of Shalmaneser, which he was not, in 1 Samuel 7.13 that the Philistines never again entered Israelite territory after the victory of Samuel, which is contradicted by the subsequent narrative. A classical case of inconsistency in historical information is the account of Joshua's campaigns in the south as recorded in Joshua 10.28–39 contrasted with the information to be found in Judges 1 which contradicts this flatly at several points. This may hardly seem worth mentioning but for the fact that, though fundamentalism of the cruder kind is practically extinct, various kinds of concordism are still popular even among scholars, perhaps American scholars in particular.

The difficulty is not so great in questions concerning the positive sciences where we expect ancient writers, including biblical writers, to be mistaken. We very sensibly accept with equanimity the fact that the Old Testament represents the earth as saucer-shaped or states that bats are birds (Lev. 11.9). They were wrong, but it does not matter, a point made by St Augustine a long time ago. This suggests that it might be useful to make a distinction between what pertains to salvation, the religious message of the Scriptures, on the one hand, and things not pertaining to salvation on the other. Such a distinction, however, has never been popular in Catholic teaching and is explicitly reprobated as recently as 1943 in *Divino Afflante Spiritu*:

> Later this solemn definition of Catholic doctrine (in Vatican I) which claims for these books "in their entirety and with all their parts" a divine authority such as must enjoy immunity from any error whatsoever, was contradicted by certain Catholic writers who dared to restrict the truth of Sacred Scripture to matters of faith and morals alone, and to consider the remainder, touching matters of the physical or historical order, as *obiter dicta* and as having (according to them) no connection whatever with faith (par. 3).

One recalls that Newman was one of those who *dared* to put forward his own version of the *obiter dicta* view, suggesting tentatively that perhaps Tobias' dog may not actually have wagged its tail but that the tail-wagging could be simply a literary device for heightening the effect of euphoria at the son's homecoming (Tob. 11.9). This view was not kindly received at the time.

This kind of solution, which distinguishes between essential and non-essential elements in the Scriptures, should be put aside at once as superficial and artificial and therefore an obstacle to a real solution in principle. With regard to this, it is rather important to understand the present position of the teaching authority, the latest statement of which comes in a sentence in the third chapter of the Constitution on Divine Revelation of Vatican II, one which, however, is of disputed interpretation. It runs as follows:

> Since, therefore, all that the inspired authors or hagiographers affirm must be regarded as affirmed by the Holy Spirit, we must in consequence hold that the books of Scripture firmly, faithfully and without error teach that truth which God, *for the sake of our salvation*, wished to confer on the Sacred Scriptures. (My italics.)

As is widely known, this was one of the several paragraphs of the council documents which was the object of a special papal intervention. The original draft affirmed that the books of Scripture faithfully and without error teach "salvific truth", *veritatem salutarem*. Fearful no doubt that this might be construed to mean that only this kind of truth fell under the divine guarantee, Paul VI had it changed to the above. The Pope's solicitude was understandable but the distinction is exiguous, to say the least. The passage is still open to the interpretation that the intention to teach salvific truth is discernible only in some parts of the Scriptures and that therefore only here does the qualification *without error* apply or, namely, to the view that "Scripture is claimed to be inerrant only for religious truth and not for statements of a scientific or historical nature" (Hans Küng writing in *The Sunday Times*, 12 December 1964). This would certainly represent a clear departure from previous teaching as contained in Vatican I, *Providentissimus Deus* (1893) and *Divino Afflante Spiritu* (1934) as quoted above.

In spite of the verbal ambiguity, however (and this is by no means the only case in this document), it was clearly not intended to teach the kind of dichotomous approach which we rejected a moment ago. What it does is very sensibly to relativize the older, more rigid view by referring truth in the Scriptures to the intention to affirm postively, with special regard to their central theme, namely the divine salvific will revealed progressively throughout history and definitely in Christ. This implies a willingness to unfreeze our categorized way of thinking and to determine as far as possible the attitude of the writer to the factuality of the events he is recording by the use of form-criticism and other techniques of literary criticism which are available.

The element of uncertainty in this whole discussion, reflected in the paragraph just quoted, is the relation of history, and the history of Israel in particular, to God's message of salvation communicated in the Scriptures. Today more than ever we are convinced that God revealed his redemptive purpose through events and that this presence within the events was first perceived and then communicated by certain individuals or groups within Israel. Perhaps we should speak not just of communication but of inter-communication. There can therefore be no dichotomy between religious truth and historical truth. The "message" is *in* the events; it has not to be extracted from them. This applies to the whole of the historical process of which the Bible is the record.

It is here that our deepened understanding of the nature of historical writing, and of Israelite historiography in particular, has affected the way we think both of biblical inspiration and inerrancy (truth). As to the first, we have to remember that the official "frozen" version of inerrancy was elaborated during the heyday of nineteenth-century historicism. History was regarded as a positive science like the natural sciences with its own object which was *the fact*. History-writing consisted in putting together a certain number of separate "atomic" facts to produce a photographically and stenographically accurate picture of a past event. This was done, ideally, in a purely objective and scientific way. The ideal historian would be, perhaps, Mommsen reconstructing an epoch of Roman history on the basis of a detailed study of inscriptions.

There is no need to expatiate in detail on the decline and disappearance of historicism. Today it is taken for granted that the subject-matter of history cannot be compared with that of the natural sciences since history deals with non-recurrent events. Facts are not like atomic particles completely independent of a knower. History cannot be completely objective in the sense of being independent of the judgment of the historian. First of all, history is a selection of facts and in order to select one must have a principle or principles of selection. This would be particularly important to bear in mind in reading the gospels since "there are also many other things which Jesus did" (Jn. 12.25). And then, a fact is only a fact for one who knows it as a fact; the very concept of "fact" implies a relation to the subject knowing, that is, the historian. Facts only emerge in the light of some presupposed agreed interpretation of the world or the historical process as a whole. This shows us how careful we have to be in talking about historical truth in the Bible. It implies at least that historical truth is not the same as the photographical reconstruction of a past event (e.g. the conquest of Canaan) by the assembly of facts. As has been rightly said, the object of biblical inerrancy is not truths in the plural but truth, religious truth, in the singular.[1]

As for the history of Israel, we have at least come to realize that before we come to problems of history we have to solve some literary problems. This involves the application of the techniques of literary criticism to the biblical texts, including the study of literary genres. This undertaking, as is well known, met initially with a distinctly cool reception from the teaching authority (*Spiritus Paraclitus*, 1920, spoke disdainfully of "so-called literary genres"), later to be positively enjoined on Catholic exegetes (in *Divino Afflante Spiritu*). We are now better able to decide what is and what is not historical writing. Jonah, Tobit and Judith belong to the category of edifying fiction or the historical novelette – a conclusion already suggested in the title of the last named which means "the Jewess". We are also more aware of the *arrière-plan* of narratives presented as historical and of the long literary and pre-literary history behind some of them. We know, to take one example, that the taking up of the ark to Jerusalem by David (2 Sam. 6) was commemorated in the liturgy and consequently have to allow for the possibility that this ark-liturgy has reflected back on the narrative as we have it. The same possibility exists for the highly stylized account of the taking of Jericho in Joshua 6 and even more so for the Exodus story which can to some extent

---

[1] I. de la Potterié, "La Verité" de la Sainte Ecriture *ou* l'Histoire du Salut d'après la Constitution dogmatique "Dei Verbum", *Nouvelle Revue Théologique*, 88 (1966), 149–69.

be regarded as an expanded form of the Passover *haggada*.

It is important, further, to bear in mind the distinction between the intention of recording an event and the representational elements used to describe it. A half-dozen slashes with a crayon can be a more faithful representation of a model than a photograph – meaning that there is more than one way of recording an event. Catholics in particular have been all too prone to ignore the interpretative function of a writer – especially in the case of the Synoptic gospels – and to expect him to represent events in the objective and photographic way found in one of the better newspapers today. Our bad old Roman Catholic habit of freezing everything, of isolating and absolutizing, of nailing our colours to the wrong masts, has not made it easy for us to penetrate below the surface and seize in all its complexity and richness the import of a historical tradition in the Scriptures. It should, for example, be obvious that the account of the conquest of Canaan in Joshua is highly stylized, theologized and even polemicized. We have all the tribes in formal array and under one leader winning hands down, going through the land with fire and (of course) the sword, arriving finally at Shiloh where they set up their central sanctuary and allot each tribe its territory with its borders exactly defined. A glance at the earlier and more realistic account in Judges 1 will warn us that it cannot really have been like this. Very often we have several traditions of different origin, each one taken by itself giving us only a partial and onesided access to the event, and in many cases we will have to confess that we just do not know what happened.

We have to remember also that there is a development within the Scriptures themselves and the Old Testament in particular. The Northern covenant-code of laws (in Ex. 20–23) is taken over, revised, interpreted and to a great extent superseded in the Deuteronomic law-code (Dt. 12–26); early traditions about Samuel and the rise of the monarchy have to be read in the light of the later, prophetic and anti-monarchic writings on the same subject; the work of the Chronicler uses the much earlier historical writings in Samuel and Kings as a source, often modifying and bringing up to date in accordance with the theological ideas of a later age. Where, for example, God tempts David to make a census in 2 Samuel 24.1, by the time of 1 Chronicles 21.1 Satan is held responsible.

Reflecting along these lines has led a German Jesuit scholar, Norbert Lohfink, to conclusions on the subject of inerrancy which some have hailed as a genuine breakthrough, others as an alarming innovation.[2] He argues that, in the light of what we know of the composition of the Old Testament, it is no longer possible to regard the individual writer as the object of inerrancy. Do we then have to say that it is the individual book which is inerrant? This would not be very meaningful either since the Bible is not a library of books but a dynamic unity which came to its complete form not by the addition of one book to another but by a process of meditating, re-thinking and re-reading what was there already and consequently of adding, re-editing, modifying in the way we have seen. Thus, whoever added Deuteronomy 4.25–31 and 30.1–10 to the book to form a final editorial stage gave a new depth of meaning and a new orientation to the rest of the book which it did not have before. Therefore each part of the Scriptures acquires its definitive sense only when the unity of the whole is complete, that is, with the final establishment of the scriptural canon. We can consequently speak of the inerrancy of any particular passage only in a relative way, is so far, that is, as it remains open to future correction, modification, neutralization or clarification. The logical conclusion is that, while the whole process from beginning to end is inspired, we should reserve inerrancy only for the final sense given to each part by the Christ-event. Putting it in a nutshell, it is not what anything in the Bible *meant* which is important, but what it *means*.

There is no space to discuss this view in detail. It has at least shown up the far too narrow basis upon which the idea of biblical inerrancy or truth has been considered up to this time, and that would be a positive contribution in itself. It has related the

[2] "Uber die Irrtumslosigkeit und die Einheit der Schrift", *Stimmen der Zeit*, 174 (1964), 161–81. There is an English summary in *Theology Digest*, 13 (1965), 185–92, and a discussion, not too favourable, by R. North in *American Ecclesiastical Review*, 152, June 1965, 367–72. Several other scholars, however, Coppens and Grelot in particular, have received it favourably.

question of truth firmly to the centre towards which everything in the Scriptures is directed, God revealing and giving himself through Christ. We shall have to leave to the reader to discuss whether there is not a danger here of vaporizing the literal sense in favour of typology and to answer the question what kind of meaning the Scriptures can continue to have for Jews to whose forebears they were first addressed. Side by side with this necessary insistence on the absolute reference to the Christ-event, must we not also think of the Scriptures as addressed to the one continuous prophetic community in successive ages and that therefore inerrancy, or whatever else we want to call it, must somehow be in function of that continuous, providentially directed community-existence?

Maybe we could end these few considerations with an analogy between inerrancy and papal infallibility. The latter begins to look somewhat different once we relate it, as we have been doing in recent years, more closely to the community in which the Spirit is present as an inspiring and directing force. The divine guarantee of this presence is given in both cases in view of the continued existence of the community throughout the ages. Maybe both terms, papal infallibility and inerrancy, are inadequate and misleading. The former is defined as an *assistentia negativa* guaranteeing somehow that the pope will not propagate error when speaking *ex cathedra* on questions concerning faith and morals. Inerrancy has likewise been defined as a negative effect of inspiration in view of the life of the community at any given time. If we extend unduly the scope and meaning of either, in the terms in which we choose to define them, we only succeed in making trouble for ourselves.

D

V

The Created World

MYTHICAL THINKING aims to impose some sort of order on the chaos of experience and at the same time control the incalculable forces which threaten orderly existence from the outside. For this it is necessary to have a fixed beginning and end to provide a context within which to think of the world and explain its present constitution. That is why so many primitive accounts of the origin of the world speak of the creation of order out of chaos rather than an absolute beginning from nothing, and this is essentially true of the origins account in the Old Testament though it does not exhaust its meaning. At the same time, it provides a means for expressing something about the life of man in the world, of giving that life meaning by placing it in contact with the sources of the world's existence. It will be clear, therefore, that these ancient creation stories are more concerned with expressing an attitude to the world and a meaning and purpose which it reveals and which can be discovered by man than a conviction about what really happened sometime in the remote past.

The first and most obvious thing to be said about Creation in the Old Testament, and in the first chapter of the Old Testament in particular, is that it is not concerned with describing an event which stands as first in a series. Not directly at any rate. As Job was to be reminded, there was no one there to witness it:

> Where were you when I laid the foundation of the earth?
> Tell me, if you have understanding.
> Who determined its measurements – surely you know!
> Or who stretched the line upon it?
> On what were its bases sunk or who laid its cornerstone,
> when the morning stars sang together
> and all the sons of God shouted for joy? (38.4–7).

Even in the late and theological account of Genesis 1 the picture is still one of the imagination: the dark waste, the abyss, the supernatural wind. A more accurate interpretation of the structure of the chapter has dealt the death-blow to any kind of concordism and no one, fortunately, is much interested nowadays in discussing whether there *could* be light before the sun or in proving *creatio ex nihilo* from a disputable parsing of the first sentence.

Historical theology demands that we place Old Testament faith in creation and a creator-God in the context of the developing faith of Israel. The earliest divine titles used do not reveal belief in a cosmic deity. In the period before Moses and the adoption of Yahwism the patriarchs appear to have worshipped different *numina*, whose titles attach them not, as was usually the case, to the forces of nature, not even to any kind of place, but to people and social groups – "the God of Abraham, Isaac and Jacob". This shows how deeply Hebrew faith was rooted in social realities and the working out of the historical destiny of specific social groups. The founding-event was political: the dissolution of political allegiance to Pharaoh, the formation of a new alliance, a promise affirmed juridically of land-tenure. The fundamental article of faith was in God as creator of a people not of the whole world.

Everyone knows how closely related are the concept of God in any age and the anthropological and cosmological suppositions of the same age. The Old Testament provides a good example of how the concept of deity evolves in response to the changing ideas of the people who have attached themselves to a particular manifestation of deity and how much it is influenced by their own internal crises. The crisis of faith set by entry into the land of Canaan arises from a conflict as to the nature of deity. What relation could Yahweh have to the Canaanite pantheon? Behind the absolute rejection of any attempt at a symbiosis by the prophets, expressed most clearly in the Elijah cycle of stories, there are signs that some attempt was made to solve the problem. Sometimes this appears in a rather naïve form, as in the Song of Moses (Dt. 32) where El, the head of the pantheon, is represented as allotting lesser tutelary gods to the various nations, including

Yahweh to Israel:

> When the Most High (el elyon) gave to the nations their
>   inheritance,
> when he separated the sons of men,
> he fixed the bounds of the peoples according to the number of
>   the sons of God.
> For Yahweh's portion is his people,
> Jacob his allotted heritage (vv.8–9).

The fact is that in Canaan there was already a creator-god. In the Ugaritic texts El (cf. Elohim, designation of deity in the Old Testament) is called "creator of creatures" and in a Phoenician inscription "creator of the earth". This would in some way have raised the problem of the relation of Yahweh to the processes of nature and of the whole cosmos. How could he fit in? How far did his power and sphere of influence extend?

There are indications in the poetical literature that from a fairly early period Yahweh was considered to have brought about the present cosmic order as the result of a great cosmogonic victory over the forces of chaos. These are represented mythologically in a way common in the ancient Near East at that time: Rahab and Leviathan (Lothan) the sea-monsters, Tannin the dragon (see Ps. 89.11; Is. 30.7; Ezek. 29.3, etc.). The suggestion has been made with some plausibility that at one stage the origins account in Genesis 2.4 ff. was preceded by a highly coloured mythological account of creation in the form of such a battle. At a later stage of theological reflection this would have been replaced by the so-called Priestly Creation-recital. If this is so, it would be a good example of the development of doctrine *within* scriptural revelation. The first chapter of Genesis as we now have it presents an extraordinary pure version of the divine creative activity. There is no vestige of conflict, much less of the creative process triggered off by copulation or even by the self-procured seed or spittle of a god as elsewhere in that area. God creates by his all-powerful word. It is sufficient for him to utter that word and the whole created order is there.

Before any idea of Yahweh as a creator-god could arise, there-

fore, certain conditions had to be fulfilled. First, the exclusive tie
which bound him to a social group and thereafter to a certain
place, the land of Canaan, had to be broken. This was achieved
through the deeper insights of the great prophets of Israel. All
these men, even before the beginning of written prophecy in the
eighth century, were interested in the problem of Yahweh's
relations with the nations which surrounded Israel and which
had a bearing on its destiny. It is no accident that the writings
of these prophetic figures began to be preserved only from the
time when the political activity of these nations began to impinge
decisively upon Israel and threaten its existence. Almost all of
them from the time of Amos contain oracles dealing with the
nations and these reveal that they thought of Yahweh's power as
extending beyond the borders of their own land. Amos states
decisively, in a well-known passage, that Yahweh had been responsible for the exodus not just of Israel from Egypt but of
Philistia from Caphtor and the Syrians from Kir (9.7). This begins
to imply that the doctrine of a creator-god was approached not
through mythical thinking as elsewhere but through the problem
of the reality of God's power in the world here and now. Creation
will answer the question not what happened *then* but what is really
happening *now* in the world.

The decisive crisis for Israel was the exile. Yahweh seemed to
have been defeated by Marduk the prestigious god of Babylon
and the question must have arisen: were his power and presence
just an illusion after all? Was he just a projection of the national
will-to-live as was, for example, Ashur of the Assyrians and
Kemosh of the Moabites? If faith, the faith of the fathers, was to
be preserved, Israel had to let the old national god die and a
new concept arise. Their thinking about God had to be related to
the immeasurably wider political and social horizon which came
within their view in their new situation. As far as we know, the
breakthrough was first achieved through the inspiration of the
anonymous prophet whose sayings have been preserved in the
second part of the book of Isaiah. It is significant that the word
which is used exclusively of the divine creative activity in the
Hebrew Bible, the verb *bara'*, occurs with great frequency in

Deutero-Isaiah and hardly at all before this time.[1] What is stressed is that the God who is the universal creator is the *God-for-Israel*. Israel must believe that they have a future, that Yahweh can create a future for them, since it is he who created the world in the first place and set Israel in it to fulfil his purpose. They must believe that the political activity of Cyrus which the prophet's contemporaries were witnessing is directed to this end since he who is the lord of history is also the universal creator (41.4 ff.; 45.1–7, 12). Here again the idea of creation arises from a certain view of world history and of the destiny of the chosen people in it at a certain time. It is also connected with the possibilities open for the future. It is not what God has done once; it is rather what he is doing all the time, combined with the idea that this action must have its source in an eternal decree concerned essentially with Israel, and must reach its end. Just as in the mythical pattern *Urzeit* is *Endzeit,* so here to the action of God in the beginning there corresponds the creation of "new heavens and a new earth" and a new Jerusalem (65.17–18).

In keeping with this the anonymous prophet closely associates creation with the exodus as the act creative of a people. This is a central theme of this part of the book. The self-annunciation of Yahweh as creator is introductory to his declaration of intention with regard to Israel:

> I am the Lord, your Holy One,
> The Creator of Israel, your King (43.15)

This is an essential element is so many Jewish prayers beginning "Blessed are thou, Adonai, king of the universe . . ." which may well go back at least in inspiration to this period. In the same way, the short hymns of praise found in Amos (e.g. 4.13) and elsewhere (Jer. 31.35–6; Is. 42.5), which are almost certainly exilic, are used antiphonally in the recital of his redemptive purpose in history. In a similar way, the opening verses of Psalm 136 which hymn the creating God serve only as an introduction to the recital of his high deeds in history. It follows that the central Old Testament doctrine is not creation but redemption. In support of

---

[1] Only in Jer. 27.5; 32.17; Dt. 4.32; Ps. 89, 13, 48; 104,30; 148.5, the date of none of which can be established with certainty.

this is the fact that wherever the thought of a creator-God and of the wonders of the created order occur independently of that of redemption there is reason to suspect a foreign influence at work, especially in the magnificent hymn to the creator-God contained in Psalm 104 which depends to some extent on the Egyptian Hymn of Ikhnaton.[2]

Only when we have grasped the origins and line of development of Old Testament thinking on creation can we understand what the New Testament says on this subject. We cannot follow this up here but simply draw attention to the unbroken line of development between the God who "created you, O Jacob, who formed you, O Israel . . . everyone who is called by my name, whom I created for my glory" (Is. 43.1–7) and the Father of Jesus Christ who "chose us in him before the foundation of the world . . . destined and appointed to live for the praise of his glory" (Eph. 1.4, 12).

If, therefore, what the Old Testament says about creation, expressed in its clearest form in Deutero-Isaiah and subsequently set out schematically and theologically in Genesis 1, is not concerned essentially with an absolute beginning or an event in the past, what is its real meaning for us today?

Creation is today generally understood to express in the first place man's dependence on God, his creatureliness. Yet if we read Genesis 1 carefully and compare it with other ancient origin-stories, the Babylonian *Enuma elish* in particular, we shall see that it says very little about man as a dependent creature. By desacralizing the whole of the natural order – the dark abyss, the heavenly bodies, the animal world worshipped by other peoples – it frees man from the servitude to divine powers and places him as a free agent in the centre of the whole created order. He is positively commanded to multiply and actualize his dominion in the world. The earth belongs to man: "the heavens are the Lord's heavens, but the earth he has given to the sons of men" (Ps. 115, 16). We certainly do not find anything of that feeling of dependence and impotence which for Schleiermacher is the basis of religion. What is stressed in the Old Testament, more than

[2] See also Ps. 19 and Gen. 14.19 with their Canaanite background.

dependence, is the precariousness of man's existence in the world. Since the world does not contain the answer to the problems which his existence in it raises he can never feel at home in it. The world reveals itself to him as not, in the last analysis, self-explanatory. He cannot exorcize his anxiety by depending on it, immersing himself in it. Other religions aimed at inserting man into the recurrent processes of nature, but for Hebrew man nature revealed a creative and purposeful will which controlled it:

> When thou hidest thy face, they are dismayed;
> when thou takest away their breath, they die
> and return to their dust.
> When thou sendest forth thy breath they are created,
> and thou renewest the face of the ground (Ps. 104.29–30).

Thus creation was not just something eternally and necessarily *there*. Since it depended on will it was conditional and even reversible. This explains why judgment is so often expressed in the prophets and most clearly in the story of the Flood as an un-creation, the positive undoing of the order established for man. This comes through clearly in a passage from Jeremiah where judgment is a progressive undoing of the order laid down at the beginning:

> I looked on the earth, and lo, it was waste and void;
> and to the heavens, and they had no light.
> I looked on the mountains, and lo, they were quaking,
> and all the hills moved to and fro.
> I looked, and lo, there was no man,
> and all the birds of the air had fled.
> I looked, and lo, the fruitful land was a desert.
> and all its cities were laid in ruins
> before the Lord, before his fierce anger (4.23–26).

Paradoxically, man's dependence, his precariousness, the fact that he is suspended between non-being and being, is the root of his freedom. Genesis 1 is really urging him not to surrender that freedom to anything in the world, not to return to the servitude from which he escaped when he was called out of the timeless mythical world into freedom. It is now only through the exercise of his freedom that the task imposed on man to "have dominion", that is, fulfil the world, can be brought about. Here again, therefore, the doctrine of creation is fundamentally soteriological, and this is how it is thought of in the New Testament. By means of a quotation from Psalm 8, a creation-hymn in praise of man, Hebrews (2.5–9) shows how the new man created in Christ is at the centre of the world and responsible for its renewal. The responsibility of creating the new heavens and new earth has been passed on to him.

What the doctrine of creation amounts to, seen from the anthropological point of view, that is, from our end (which is the only end we can see it from), is that our existence in the world has a meaning, a whence and a whither. The old cosmogonies which lie behind Genesis 1 had the purpose of imposing a meaning on life, especially social life. They were the affirmation of faith in such a meaning, a faith which was constantly renewed by the recital of the creation-myth, for example in Babylonia at the New Year Festival. The creation-recital of Genesis was no doubt also read and listened to as a return to this source of meaning by re-attaching man to the roots of his life in the cosmos and to the will and life of God who upheld it. Hence the importance for the Christian of the creation-recital in the Easter vigil by means of which we return, in the word and the suggestive images which communicate it, to this vital centre. We misrepresent the Genesis creation-recital if we read it as the description of an event or as a demonstration. It is an affirmation, and at the same time an invitation, an invitation to participate here and now in the creative process which our existence in the world reveals to us.

VI

The Original Meaning of Original Sin

Perhaps no subject in the whole range of systematic theology arouses so much doubt, confusion and diffidence today as that of Original Sin. Does the Old Testament really speak "of man's *first* disobedience"? Is this the way St Paul understands it when he speaks of sin coming into the world "through one man"? Is the Church committed to the view that the first man, whose name was Adam, committed a sin which he passed on by heredity to all the human race which followed him?

The first, most important and most difficult step is to find out what the Old Testament, and Genesis chapter 3 in particular, is speaking about. The story of what happened in the garden is part of a continuous recital which goes from creation to the call addressed by God to Abraham. As almost all admit nowadays, it is the result of a basic narrative, put together perhaps as early as the reign of Solomon, which was re-edited with additions (and no doubt subtractions) by the scribes and priests of the post-exilic period. Both of course make use of much older material of the most diverse kind, including myth. We have therefore the complex problem of deciding what the story could have meant, presuming that it was not invented by the Basic Narrator, before he took it over; what it meant as taken over by him and placed in the total context of his work; what it meant in the still wider context of the final form in which we now have these first chapters of the Bible.

No one can doubt, to begin with, that the biblical writers have made use of myths current in the cultural environment of their own and an earlier time. The tree of life, the snake, the cherub with the thunderbolt are only some of the mythical motifs familiar in that milieu. Ezekiel's lament on the king of Tyre also makes use of the myth of the godly being "full of wisdom, perfect in beauty" who was "in Eden, in the garden of God" (Ezek. 28.13). It should not be forgotten that a little later on in the Basic Narrative we find what is in effect another account of a Fall, and presented in an even more explicitly mythological fashion. In Genesis 6.1-4 the corruption of mankind is attributed to the intermarriage between divine beings and human women. Almost certainly this is a fragment from a longer origins-story which once existed independently. Then again, and connected with this, there is the question of a pre-existent, pre-cosmic evil, referred to in Christian doctrine generally as the Fall of the Angels, which is also represented mythically. In Isaiah's taunt against Babylon the city is addressed as "Day Star (Lucifer), son of Dawn" who has fallen from heaven (Is. 14.12). "Day Star" and "Dawn" are lesser gods in Canaanite mythology who rebel unsuccessfully against El, the high-god of the pantheon. There is no question, therefore, that the whole *arrière-fond* of what the Old Testament says about the origins of evil is mythical, but this does not solve the problem of what use is made of mythical representations in the new context of understanding created by the biblical writers.

The Basic Narration (more commonly called the Yahwist corpus) tells a fairly straightforward story. It presumes creation – the heavens and the earth are already *there* – but there can be no civilized life since there was no man to harness the abundant water-supply to make the land fertile. So God created man and commanded him to till the garden in which he was placed. He is given free access to everything in creation except the tree of the knowledge of good and evil. Despite man's close kinship with the animal world, no adequate companion can be found for him there so God creates woman from man. She it is who falls prey to the temptation of the Snake and the first result of this is the experience of shame. The punishment of death is not carried out at once but the man and woman are driven out of the garden where their first two children are born. There follows the fratricide. The tainted line of Cain continues but Seth is born to take the place of the murdered Abel.

As we have suggested, there are good reasons to believe that the Yahwist corpus was put together during the early monarchy, probably during the reign of Solomon. There are some striking similarities in style and expression between Genesis 3 and some parts of the lively narrative about David and the struggle for succession to his throne – the title "Yahweh God" used only here, "to know good and evil", the lively and psychologically revealing use of dialogue. More important still is the resemblance in theme. David's sin with Bathsheba involves a sentence of death passed by God which, however, is not carried out (2 Sam. 12.13). Instead, their child dies and there follows the murder of one brother by another. The son born in place of the dead child is the one through whom the dynasty and the promise is carried on, as Seth takes the place of the murdered Abel (Gen 4.25). The story of the woman of Tekoa, hired by the crafty Joab to win pardon for Absalom, is a kind of fictionalization of the fratricide and its consequences and comes very close thematically and even verbally to the description of the fratricide and its consequences in Genesis 4 (see 2 Sam. 14). Particularly noticeable is the emphasis in the David-history on disobedience which takes the form of a sexual sin: David with Bathsheba in disobedience to the covenant under which the king also existed, Amnon's rape of his half-sister Tamar (2 Sam. 13), Absalom's rebellion against his father made final in the occupation of his harem and intercourse with the concubines the king has left behind (2 Sam. 16), Adonijah's coveting of the Shunammite maiden (1 Kings 2.17). In the case of the three sons of the king this action led to death. While the sin in Genesis 3 is explicitly one of disobedience, the form it takes is quite clearly sexual.

Confirmation of this can be found in the first nine chapters of Proverbs attributed to Solomon. Though redacted long after the time of Solomon in their final form, there is no reason why the greater part of the material we find here should not go back to the time of the early monarchy, especially if we compare it with wisdom writings from Egypt like the Wisdom of Anu from the same time. The theme of these chapters is that true wisdom consists in fidelity to the covenant and the commandments of God. They are concerned to show some false leads in the search for life, knowledge and happiness. Above all, a man must keep himself free from the loose and adventurous woman, dexterous with words, who can lead him to look in the wrong direction for the satisfaction of his desires and to listen to whom, leads to death. These chapters have clear affinity not only with the experience of David and Solomon, the latter of whom we are told loved many foreign women who led him into idolatry and apostasy; they have a definite thematic connection with the story that stands at the beginning of the Yahwist work. Portrayed is the man who loses all through the wiles of the woman, and we also find the tree of life (3.18) and read of the foolish "eating the fruit of their way" (1.31). In 6.29–31 there is a reference to the sin of David represented in the parable of Nathan as stealing, and indeed the whole section is addressed to the crown-prince, the successor to the throne.

To have established this context for our understanding of Genesis 3 is very important since we cannot really go further with the discussion on Original Sin until we have got the first stage right. Far from being a primitive and artless story, it is a highly sophisticated composition which we should place in the category of wisdom-writing. In the Yahwist work and the writings about David and the succession struggle culminating in Solomon we can watch the development from plain history-writing through various attempts to fictionalize a historical situation as the story of the woman of Tekoa and the parable of Nathan (2 Sam. 12), to the different attempts to universalize the experience of the early monarchy in Israel found in Proverbs 1–9 and Genesis 3–4. What we have originally is a warning about a false sense of power and autonomy, a false search for a power and knowledge independent of the will of the covenant-God, which was only too well exemplified in Israel's first kings. The role of the Woman and the Snake, in Canaan the symbol of secret and magical knowledge, are brilliantly to the point seen in this context.

Genesis 3–4 reflects therefore one of the supreme crises in the spiritual history of the People of God.

But, of course, the message is not confined to kings. The same danger beset the Israelites from the first days of their settlement in Canaan. There are warnings against the dangers of inter-marriage with the native populations throughout the earlier part of the Old Testament. Ezekiel is commanded to tell Jerusalem, that is, Israel, "your father was an Amorite and your mother a Hittite" (chapter 16) and in the parable which follows all the subsequent evils are traced back to this marriage with a foreign woman. It would seem that the narrative of Genesis 3 fits in here in referring to a danger not just for the king but the people as a whole in intermarrying with non-Israelite elements which would normally imply the acceptance of the cults practised by these foreigners. It would therefore be a sort of paradigm of temptation and fall for Israel in her life in the land.

But the outlook of the writer takes in very much more than the horizons of Israel or the first few decades of the millennium when the monarchy was set up. The protagonist is called simply "the Man" throughout – there is no certain occurrence of the word as a proper name, Adam, until the birth of Seth in 4.25. Similarly his partner is simply "the Woman" until after the sin is committed. This in itself shows the intention of giving universal significance to what was in fact conceived of within a precisely limited context in time and place. Moreover, the story occurs in the survey from creation to the call of Abraham which has the purpose of showing the kind of world in which Israel was given her mission and why salvation was necessary. Precisely by being placed in this context it is made into a paradigm of *la condition humaine*. "The Man" is Everyman of the medieval morality play; in fact, you and me.

It is interesting to note that the Adam story is hardly ever heard of again in the Old Testament. There are broken remnants here and there in the poetic literature of a paradisal state when man and nature were in harmony and there was no violence on the earth. In Isaiah 11.6–9 and 65.25 we have the statement, based on a mythical view of history, that the end-age will be like the beginning, with the wild animals tame and living in peace together;

and in the latter we hear of the serpent eating dust. The same mythical representation is found among the Sumerians who located the paradise-land in Dilmun at the mouth of the Two Rivers. Other peoples held similar beliefs in antiquity. There is no reference anywhere in the Hebrew Old Testament to an original sin of Adam. Deuteronomy traces back the original sin of Israel to the defection of the monarchy, especially the act of Jeroboam in setting up an apostate cult in the Northern Kingdom. Later Jewish tradition, followed by some of the Fathers of the Church, looks rather to the intermarriage of heavenly beings with earthly women as the beginning of evil among men. We do find, in writings in the inter-testamentary period, and in the later rabbis, speculations of a fantastic nature on the first man and the preternatural gifts which he enjoyed – his enormous dimensions, for example. But there is no doctrine of Original Sin as such in Judaism which passed over by a natural transition to early Christianity. Judaism was and is remarkably optimistic about the innate goodness of man and stresses much more that he is in the image of God than his tendency to evil.

If we had to summarize the real, theological meaning for the Old Testament and Judaism of the story in Genesis 3 we should have to see it in the light of the covenant which bound the people and their God together. Their God was not a forbidding and distant deity but a God-for-Israel, God-for-man. The covenant by which God came near to his people was the only way in which Israel could think of man's relationship to God at any time and in any circumstances. And so he creates the first man, puts him in a garden, converses familiarly with him and, to point out the way to life and happiness, gives him a command. This is in keeping with the Israelite's attitude to the commands inherent in the covenant; they were a gift leading to life and wisdom, not an imposition. The only kind of sin in this context could be a rejection of this offer, this nearness of God. Just as Deuteronomy sees the exile of Israel from the land as the result of covenant-disobedience, so the first man disobeys and is cast out from the garden. There is also the fact that sin is shown in the prehistoric period from the first man to the first Hebrew, Abraham, as a disruption of human community: that between man and woman, the tribal community of the desert (Lamech), the community of nations (tower of Babel). The dispersion of tongues is seen as the climax of this breakdown of community between men. The covenant, on the contrary, was seen right from the beginning as the means of creating a genuine human community out of the most disparate elements. Common fidelity to the covenant-demands is seen as the cement of social unity.

It should be clear from the foregoing that to reduce the disobedience of the first man as presented in Genesis 3 to an original sin passed on by biological descent to all who came after would not only be far from the intention of the original writers but would also greatly impoverish the message which is here being conveyed to us. It is as misleading and, in fact, impossible to prove that all men descend from "Adam" as it is to try to prove that all Israelites descended from Jacob = Israel. That all mankind forms a unity is a conclusion which only modern science has been able to formulate and defend satisfactorily. What we have in the apparently simple story in Genesis is an intuition reached, at a deeper and richer level, of the solidarity of all mankind, and indeed of the whole created order, in a common destiny and of the only obstacles which can stand in the way of its fulfilment.

VII

On Reading Deuteronomy

FOR MANY CHRISTIANS there will probably be something rather odd if not amusing about being invited to read the Book of Deuteronomy. For one thing it has the initial disadvantage of an uncouth and barely pronounceable title, quite apart from the fact that in any case the word is a mistranslation. Then the first-time reader, speculatively turning the pages and lighting on the prohibition of boiling a kid in its mother's milk or eating camel flesh, and never having been tempted to do either, might be forgiven for wondering how it could in any way be relevant for him. Yet it can be stated confidently that the study of this book in recent decades has played a major role in our deepening understanding of the nature and mission of the Church and consequently of inter-Church relations.

A first test of its importance is the profound influence it has had on the New Testament. Sometimes this is obvious and explicit, as in the three quotations from the book in the Temptation scene in the gospel or the saying of Jesus about the greatest commandment of the Law with reference to Deuteronomy 6.4–9, the *Shema*. More often it is at the deeper level of allusion and inference, as in the texts which speak of the covenant – including the institution of the Eucharist – community rules, Luke's sermon on a level place with its blessings and curses, the teaching on the Two Ways (see Dt. 30.15) and the like. Sometimes it is so casual that it could pass undetected: Moses' fast on the mountain forty days and nights (Dt. 9.18), Moses on the mountain being shown the land spread out at his feet as far as the Great Sea (Dt. 34.1 ff.). Or one might compare a text like the following:

The secret things belong to the Lord our God; but the things that are revealed belong to us and to our children for ever, that we may put into practice all the words of this law (Dt. 29.29).

with

Thou hast hidden these things from the wise and understanding and revealed them to babes; yea, Father, for such was thy gracious will (Mt. 11.25–6).

If we wish to grasp the real relevance of Deuteronomy, the first thing to note is that it comes to us in the form of a discourse or sermon of Moses to the laity. Not that Moses wrote this himself – which would incidentally include a circumstantial report of his own death and burial. It represents rather a precipitate of the faith of the covenant-community in many successive generations which, however, looks back all the time to the first and prototypal encounter with God at the time of Moses. It is within this homiletic framework that the law is set (chapters 12 to 26). The laity which is addressed and which takes upon itself to observe the law is the church of Israel gathered together in liturgical assembly. It is this assembly of the Lord, the *qehal Yahweh*, which becomes "the church of God" in the New Testament. This "church" in Deuteronomy is not an abstract concept. It is a concrete reality, the community actualized, realized in plenary assembly. The word *qahal* is used not just of the objective assembly but in the active sense of the coming together, the formation of the assembly: ". . . the words which the Lord spoke to you on the mountain on the day of the assembly" (9.10 and 10.4, cf. in the Greek Bible "the day of the church"). The Deuteronomist church is a reality at the same time sociological and liturgical, secular and sacred.

The fact that the people came together to renew the covenant takes us back to the first and paradigmatic encounter with God on the sacred mountain – "the day that you stood before the Lord your God at Horeb" (4.10). This is the pattern for all the assemblies which follow. But the prototypal event of Horeb-Sinai is not reconstructed on the basis of historical information about what actually happened on a specific occasion but is described as a covenant-renewal ceremony of the kind with which the Israelites were familiar during or after the settlement in Canaan. This would be particularly true of the covenant relationships of the incoming Israelites with the population around Shechem, and Shechem is evidently the focal point for covenant-making in Deuteronomy. In much the same way Luke describes Pentecost in terms of a Christian liturgical assembly, and we know from Qumran that this feast was associated with covenant-renewal at the time of Christ. This liturgical purpose explains the frequently heard call to remember "the signs and wonders" which God did for his people in Egypt and when he brought them out from there "with a mighty hand and an outstretched arm", when he redeemed them from the house of slavery (7.8). The new covenant-people has also received the command to "do this as my memorial service" (Lk. 22.19; 1 Cor. 11.24), to remember "the mighty works and wonders and signs which God did through him" (Acts 2.22). Surprisingly it is often overlooked, especially in the received dogmatic approach to theology, how the Christian understanding of redemption in its primitive social aspect is tied up intimately with the creation of a real community as the result of the great act of rescue in the Exodus. This is one of the basic themes of this book.

It is precisely here, in the social dimension of religious commitment, that a study of Deuteronomy can be most rewarding. The Deuteronomist addresses a people conscious of one shared history which gives them an unbreakable link of unity. "You are a people holy to the Lord your God. The Lord your God has chosen you for his possession out of all the peoples that are on the face of the earth" (7.6). It deals, naturally, with various offices and ministries within the community and we are aware in reading it of the tensions between the inner reality, making the community what it is, and the institutional patterns. The same in the history of the Christian Church. What is stressed here more than anything else, however, is the community itself as an indivisible unity at the same time priestly and prophetic. It is the appreciation of this insight which has so enriched our ecclesiology in recent years, more than any other single factor.

The covenant made by God with a people is *the* basic category of the Christian religion and its Scriptures as can be seen in the division into Old and New Testament (covenant). Deuteronomy deals precisely with covenant-making and covenant-renewal. Recent studies of political alliances or covenants in the Ancient Near East, especially disparity treaties between the Hittite kings and their subject states, have given us a clearer idea of the essential structure of a covenant ceremony. Such treaties generally begin with an introduction in which the king gives his names and titles and rehearses the past relations between himself and his vassal in order to emphasize his benevolence towards the vassal and thereby provide grounds for trust in entering into this new relationship. Then there follow the stipulations, often stressing the exclusive nature of the bond by forbidding foreign alliances. There are usually provisions for placing the treaty in the temple or some holy place and for reading it publicly from time to time. The agreement is then sanctioned with more or less stereotyped blessings and curses endorsed by the contracting parties.

All these elements are found in the covenant ceremony of Deuteronomy. The historical prologue in the opening chapters; Yahweh who introduces himself as he who "brought you out of the land of Egypt, out of the house of bondage" (5.6); the placing of the book beside the ark of the covenant (31.26); the order to read it publicly and liturgically (31.10–13); the curses and blessings (27–28). All this might appear to make for a legalistic and authoritarian pattern with the emphasis on law-observance and enforcement, but it is just here that the analogy cannot be pressed for Deuteronomy, we must remember, is also the heir of the great prophets of the eighth century, especially Hosea, and is full of the awe and majesty of the divine choice. The covenant is a gift, not an imposition:

> For ask now of the days that are past, which were before you, since the day that God created man upon the earth, and ask from one end of heaven to the other, whether such a great thing as this has ever happened or was ever heard of. Did any people ever hear the voice of a god speaking out of the midst of the fire, as you have heard, and still live? Or has any god ever attempted to go and take a nation for himself from the midst of another nation, by trials, by

signs, by wonders, and by war, by a mighty hand and an outstretched arm, and by great terrors, according to all that the Lord
your God did for you in Egypt before your eyes? . . . Out of heaven
he let you hear his voice because he loved your fathers and chose
their descendants after them (4.32–7).

It was not because you were more in number than any other people
that the Lord set his love upon you and chose you, for you were
the fewest of all peoples; but it is because the Lord loves you, and is
keeping the oath which he swore to your fathers, that the Lord has
brought you out with a mighty hand and redeemed you from the
house of bondage (7.7–8).

What great nation is there that has a god so near to it as the Lord
our God is to us, whenever we call upon him? (4.7).

The covenant-law, we repeat, is not a burden but a gift. Its
observance is not the task of a slave but an attempt to match the
supreme freedom in self-giving and commitment of the God who
first enters into and creates the relationship. We should recall that
Hosea had already spoken of this in terms of the most intimate
relationship of man and woman in marriage. Love and covenant-
commitment were not only inseparable but identical:

I, the Lord your God, am a jealous God . . . showing steadfast love
to thousands of those who love me and keep my commandments
(5.9–10).

You shall therefore love the Lord your God, and keep his charge,
his statutes, and his commandments (11.1).

If you love me, you will keep my commandments (Jn. 14.15).

The community comes together to hear God's word. It is
because this word is understood as the means of God's total self-
revelation and self-giving that the moral demands of the covenant
can be met, just as between man and woman any sacrifice can be
met once the mutual love is total and secure. Deuteronomy is full
of this absolute assurance that God continues to reveal, that is,
give himself to the believing community when it comes together
to listen to his word. To obey is to respond actively to God as
present:

For this commandment which I command you this day is not too hard for you, neither is it far off. It is not in heaven, that you should say, "Who will go up for us to heaven, and bring it to us, that we may hear it and do it?" Neither is it beyond the sea, that you should say, "Who will go over the sea for us, and bring it to us, that we may hear it and do it?" But the word is very near you; it is in your mouth and in your heart, so that you can do it (30.11-14).

Here we have a valuable insight into the meaning of revelation. The Word is not a word unless addressed to a subject capable of response and dialogue. The Hebrew with his intuitive and unitary view of personality thought of speech between two persons not so much as the communication of ideas but rather in the first place as a mutual recognition. When therefore God speaks he does not so much express ideas as express himself, and by so doing creates a "thou" with whom dialogue is possible. This living word was not just spoken once for all on Horeb. It is spoken whenever the community comes together and in so doing realizes its identity: "Not with our fathers did the Lord make this covenant, but with us, who are all of us alive this day" (5.3).

Deuteronomy is of special interest for us especially at this juncture of the Church's history in that it was drawn up as a programme for reform. The fact that, in some way, it lies behind the religious and political reforms of king Josiah in 622 B.C. (this can be read about in 2 Kings 22-23) has been a pivotal point of the study of the Pentateuch since the beginning of last century. This reform was radical in that it asked the kind of questions which human indolence prefers so often to pass over: where in the past did we go wrong? how can we reverse the process, go back and undo what has been badly done before going forward again? Reading Deuteronomy in the light of the historical circumstances of that time, we can see that it implies the rejection of religion conceived as a means of coercing God to one's own private advantage, getting leverage on God, and put in its place this emphasis on free commitment to the covenant-God and the community of which one formed a part.

Deuteronomy is also, finally, an ecumenical document. Everything points to its having been put together as an attempt to heal the wound of disunity between the Southern kingdom and their brethren in the North. This was in the years immediately preceding the destruction of Jerusalem, the last and short-lived resurgence of national and religious spirit, when it seemed a distinct possibility to bring together the divided provinces under one rule and one religious principle. Put together by a Judaean hand, this "edition" of the book incorporated the theological insights of a tradition different from that current in the South and made practical proposals for reintegrating the ministries of the North into that of the central shrine of Jerusalem. We do not know what course history would have taken if this radical attempt at reform and ecumenical effort had not been swept away with the young king's death at Megiddo. It was revived again as a blueprint for a new beginning by the Israelite "church" in exile and, though to a large extent submerged during the post-exilic period down to the time of Christ, was always the ideal for the chosen community. It remains so today.

VIII

Law and Community in the Pentateuch

THE TERM "Pentateuch", which is Greek for "five jars", would be intelligible for those who knew that the ancients sometimes kept their libraries in jars (and who also knew Greek) but is not very enlightening as to its content. The Jews call the whole hetero-geneous collection *torah* (law) and the five individual books "the five fifths of the law" though the division into books is secondary and can be misleading. There are two points to be made serially before going on. The first is the often overlooked fact that the Pentateuch is not a history book but a law book – that is why it is called *hattorah*, the law. The second is that *torah* has a wider meaning than our word "law". It is, like this latter, "a body of enacted or customary rules recognized by a community as binding" (*Concise Oxford Dictionary*) but it includes also the motivation for its own observance which is to be found in the context in which *torah* is presented. *Torah,* therefore, corresponds also to "re-velation" as well as "law"; we might in consequence define it as "revelational decision".

If it is true that the Pentateuch has to do essentially with law we might begin by looking at the actual law-codes which it contains, especially since most people who, full of good will, set themselves to read the Pentateuch, usually get bogged down in the Garden of Eden and go no further. Since the Pentateuch is the outcome of a long process of oral and written tradition, the laws which it contains have to be studied as resulting from a continuous, dynamic process of adaptation and reinterpretation to meet the changing circumstances of social life. The earliest code, usually called the Covenant-code, is that contained in

Exodus 20–23 reflecting on the whole a semi-nomadic way of life in the process of adaptation to an agrarian economy and containing some very ancient and rather off-putting ritual taboos and the so-called law of retaliation – life for life, eye for eye, tooth for tooth. Its most important provision is the absolute prohibition of idolatry. This body of law may well go back to the Mosaic period or shortly after. The law-code embedded in Deuteronomy (12–26) comes in its present form, in all probability, from the seventh century, as long after the time of Moses as we are distant from the Middle Ages, though it contains some very ancient legislation and is authenticated by being attributed to Moses. It represents a distinct advance on the old covenant-law and even neutralizes some of its enactments – an interesting case of the development of doctrine and morals within revelation. The ritual law-book in Leviticus, of limited interest for us today, was put together at the time of Ezekiel while the so-called Priestly Code, scattered throughout Exodus, Leviticus and Numbers, reached its final form only in the post-exilic period.

As long as this mass of criminal, constitutional and religious legislation was the only body of law known to us from Ancient Near Eastern antiquity, it was possible to make all sorts of claims for it as being unique and revolutionary. Beginning with the discovery of the Hammurapi Code in 1901, however, the archaeologists have provided us with over half-a-dozen complete or fragmentary law codes from the Semitic or Hittite areas of the Ancient Near East. Read against the background of this comparative material, the pentateuchal legislation cannot be construed as embodying a revolutionary ethos. There are certainly some humanitarian provisions in the Deuteronomic Code but these would have to be balanced against the injunction to liquidate the populations of Canaan (even though this was more of a theological retrojection from a later age to that of the Conquest) and the death penalty for striking one's parents.

The question is bound to be asked at this stage whether at least the Ten Commandments hold a unique and privileged place. It was fairly common to arrange laws in decades – there are other examples of this in the Pentateuch itself. As for the *Ten Words* as they are called in the texts, there may well have been originally more than ten and there are, at any rate, clear signs that they were not laid down once and for all. They have come down to us in two versions, one in Deuteronomy 5 the other in the Priestly recension in Exodus 20, both of which, however, go back to an earlier form. Originally all ten "words" would have been of the apodictic type ("Thou shalt not . . .") and have been developed homiletically in different ways. So, for example, sabbath observance is enjoined in Deuteronomy 5 for humanitarian reasons, in Exodus 20 on strictly theological grounds. All of the prohibitions, with the crucial exception of the prohibition of idolatry, can be found in the law codes of other groups.

There is also, at first sight, nothing very special about the religious context in which the law is placed. Deuteronomy shows us Yahweh writing the law himself and then handing it to Moses for promulgation. He commands it to be put near the ark and provision to be made for its public reading at stated intervals of time. But it was quite common for ancient people to authenticate and sanction their legislation by the pious fiction that the laws had been dictated by a deity and given to the king, priest or other religious leader. The stele of Hammurapi in the Louvre shows us the god handing the law-code to the king, having presumably written it himself. This was a necessity of social order and there is no reason to suppose that the case was different in Israel.

We can take this a stage further. Law in the Pentateuch is presented within the framework of a covenant between Yahweh and his people. It is true that we have no certain parallel to this type of relationship, though there is something approaching it among the Sumerians and in the mention of the *baal-* or *el-berit* (the lord or god of the covenant) at Shechem (Jdg. 9.4, 46). But recent studies of covenants or treaties in the Ancient Near East lead us to conclude that at some stage the Hebrews took over the language of international relationships and borrowed terms from what we would call international law to express the peculiarity of their relationship with Yahweh and the obligations arising from it. It is sometimes forgotten, however, by those who exploit this possibility of comparison, that the primitive religion of the "fathers" or patriarchs already showed this rather exceptional note of a god tied not to a particular locality or shrine but to the existence and destiny of a social group, as was shown by Albrecht Alt in his monumental essay on "The God of the Fathers" (1929). It is here rather than directly to the covenant that we have to look for the roots of that unique interest in social and political events which marks the Old Testament and the Jewish (and of course Christian) tradition. A more detailed account of the covenant-model has been dealt with elsewhere;[1] here we should note that motivation for law-observance is provided by the cultic recitation in the ceremony of covenant-making and covenant-renewal of the deeds of Yahweh with regard to his people, especially his deed of grace in the Escape – in fact it is this latter which gives him his character as *God for Israel*: "I am the Lord your God who led you out of the land of Egypt, out of the house of bondage" (Dt. 5.6; Ex. 20.2). The very nature of their god was defined with reference to political and social realities – political emancipation, repudiation of allegiance, transference of ownership.

A provisional conclusion is beginning to emerge at this stage. The *torah* is unique neither in coming miraculously into existence at a given point of time, nor in embodying a revolutionary ethic, nor in being stated in new categories. It reflects social experience over a long period and is presented in political and legal categories familiar in the world of that time. How then, we must go on to ask, could it have come to stand at the beginning of a great religious tradition common to Jew and Christian? Why was it ever "canonized" in the first place?

In seeking for a solution, let us begin on firm ground by noting that the Scriptures connect the law with the emancipation and escape of an enslaved group in Egypt. This event is described (in the first part of Exodus) not in sober historical prose but in the high style of saga embellished with poetic material (for example, the Song of Miriam in Ex. 5). It has also been deeply influenced by commemorative liturgies, especially the Passover liturgy through which a good part of the narrative has clearly been filtered. There is no reason to doubt, for all this, that something

[1] See the essay "On Reading Deuteronomy", pp. 57ff.

remarkable did happen somewhere in the region of the Nile delta in the thirteenth century and scholars have had little difficulty in showing how the biblical record fits in well enough with the admittedly scanty documentation from this period when a wave of xenophobia swept Egypt after the expulsion of the hated Hyksos. This does not imply, however, that the Escape was unique; this kind of situation could easily occur in a politically unstable age and Amos flatly denies that the Israelite exodus was the only one:

> Are you not like the Ethiopians to me, O people of Israel?
> Did I not bring up Israel from the land of Egypt,
> and the Philistines from Caphtor
> and the Syrians from Kir? (9.7)

So far, therefore, we have at the origins of the tradition the language of international politics, social legislation, political emancipation – in short, the play of social and political forces which still govern human existence. It is not going too far to say (with Harvey Cox) that the whole thing began with a massive act of civil disobedience or (with John Robinson) with someone organizing a bricklayers' strike. But how could this have started off a great religious tradition or indeed have had any particular religious significance in the first place?

Once again, we must seek an answer in the connection between Escape and Covenant. This escape was one of many, agreed, but it *revealed* something to those who took part in it. The story is familiar. It begins with the voice from the burning bush which says: "I have seen the misery of my people!" – and as yet there was no people and the speaker was nameless! He whose name might not be spoken and whom no image could represent called this bunch of slaves out of servitude into freedom. They could become a people only by becoming *his* people. Then follows the defeat of the tutelary gods behind the throne of the Pharaoh and the repudiation of allegiance to the divine monarchy which meant opting out of a whole divine cosmic system, out of an unchanging order into the unpredictable course of history. This is what Harvey Cox calls, in *The Secular City,* "the desacralization of politics". In Exodus the covenant-making at Sinai follows soon after the escape. About these chapters there are still many unsolved problems. There is certainly no attempt made here to describe a real event which took place at Sinai. Many of the elements in the description are *theologoumena,* retrojections from the covenant liturgy in Canaan, especially at Shechem. But the connection between escape and covenant is crucial just the same – there could be no covenant without escape. The escape is the result of a dynamic new faith by which all other bonds, both sacred and profane, were repudiated. It is sealed in the covenant precisely because the covenant is the free association of those who have perceived the real meaning of the event. As the American Old Testament scholar George Mendenhall puts it:

> The symbolization of historical events was possible because each group which entered the covenant community could and did see the analogy between bondage and exodus and their own experience. . . .

and he continues a little later:

> Religion in its formative period was simultaneously a bond between persons in an intolerable situation and a way of life. In a period of traditionalism it becomes merely a way of worship and a part of the total situation which makes life intolerable[2]

– meaning, I take it, that the history of the Jews in the Old Testament, especially in the nomistic period, is a good example of how revolutionaries in search of independence often enslave themselves over again by absolutizing the symbols of their freedom.

It is crucially important for our understanding of the meaning of community in the Judaeo-Christian tradition to grasp that it was initially and always remains ideally an association of free men (originally freed-men) who have repudiated or, if you wish, relativized all other ties. In keeping with this, *redemption* in scriptural terms means basically the same as community-building. Yahweh redeemed Israel in the very act of making them into a people. Exodus *is* redemption. One is redeemed *into* the people.

[2] *Biblical Archaeologist,* 25 (1962), 66 ff.

At this juncture we return to our starting-point in the law. We saw that the only really unique element was the absolute prohibition of idols. This is found in the primitive covenant-code (Ex. 20.23), is first of the Ten Words (Ex. 20.3-6; Dt. 5.7-10) and is reiterated throughout. The Lord's name itself may not be pronounced and it is quite possible that the enigmatic reply to Moses – the I AM WHO I AM of Exodus 3.14 – is in fact a refusal to give a name. This is not the case earlier when the patriarchs, before and after entering Canaan, worshipped different manifestations of deity of whom the god of Abraham, the "Kinsman" of Isaac, the "Champion" of Jacob were but three.[3] Moses himself lived as an Egyptian and no doubt worshipped as one (his name means in Egyptian "son of a [god]" though the actual name has been suppressed). It is only with the escape and the new bond with one overlord that we have a community which cuts itself off decisively from the mythical system and the servitude to divine (political) powers and launches itself into an unknown future. With this went a liberation from political ideologies – *Pharaoh is a man and not god!* This decisive act, which Max Weber calls *the disenchantment of nature,* is basic to our understanding of the Pentateuch as a whole.

It has been found surprising that the word *covenant* (*berith*) occurs only a couple of times in the pre-exilic prophets. The fact is, however, that these prophets are full of the idea of the covenant and the ethic of social involvement which it brought with it. At the same time, they speak out against the perversion of the covenant into a general religious truth which could then serve as an umbrella for social irresponsibility by permitting a return to the timeless mythical world which they had left, this time in the form of the magical supernaturalism of Canaan, essentially a *do ut des* type of religion.

We saw a moment ago that the Escape revealed something to those who took part in it. This interpretation is contained principally in Exodus but is thematic throughout the Scriptures.

---

[3] See Alt's essay, "The God of the Fathers", in *Essays on Old Testament History and Religion,* Blackwell, 1966, pp. 3–66, and W. F. Albright, *From the Stone Age to Christianity,* Johns Hopkins Press 1957,[2] pp. 247 ff.

Of course, we can easily imagine that the Egyptian interpretation, had they recorded it, would have been somewhat different. They might have referred, in the manner of political news bulletins, to a regrettable incident that took place in the region of Qantara, that their troops were experiencing some difficulty in negotiating the difficult terrain, and so on. We have no way of *proving* that the Hebrew interpretation was the only possible or correct one, and in fact the Bible is not particularly interested in proving anything. They interpreted it as a summons to accept the risks of an historical existence and undertake a journey. This is expressed in the covenant in which the break away from the static divine world of myth into freedom is expressed both as the freedom of Yahweh as a personal god not a life-force, a freedom which is communicated to the people as will (law), and that of the community which freely enters into this new relationship. The greatness of the Judaeo-Christian tradition lies in this involvement in and openness to a creative process within history and its commitment to the attainment of freedom in the fullest possible sense. Its danger lies in representing man's response as the fulfilment of an elaborate code of laws to which an absolute sanction is attached which can (and in fact did) lead to Pharisaism and spiritual slavery.

Here we must return once again to our starting-point in the relation between law and revelation. In the biblical understanding, revelation is primarily through events. The Greeks saw the world as the embodiment of a principle which must be sought beyond it – whether it be the *idea* of Plato, the *logos* of the Stoics or the *nous* of Anaxagoras. Revelation thus implied the discovery of what *is* behind what *seems to be*. The essential in the biblical view, on the contrary, is not to be found in what always *is* but in what *happens*.[4] This implies the far-reaching conclusion that the historical process contains in some way what is ultimately real and that salvation or redemption, or whatever we wish to call what the biblical revelation offers, cannot consist in an escape from the historical process but in the fulfilment of its meaning. This is true even, true especially, of eschatological thinking in

[4] See the essay "Rethinking Revelation", pp. 16 ff.

the Bible. If the Pentateuch has one central message or *kerygma* it must either be this or at least leave room for it.

The tradition contained in the Pentateuch is revitalized and re-interpreted in the prophets. The history of Israel came to be written as a public confession of failure to live out the primal experience, which in its turn is interpreted prophetically as if God had learned from the history the necessity of evil and the need for a deeper involvement. For the Christian, the Escape retains its paradigmatic value in revealing what God always does when he acts – in effecting this passage from slavery to freedom, death to life – and therefore what he does in the death-to-life of Jesus. The covenant-community is renewed at a deeper level in the table-fellowship of the Eucharist by which the community accepts the pattern and makes it part of its existence. This too looks forward to a renewed free association, open to all, one in which God's final purpose in history can be brought about.

IX

Community Models in the Pentateuch

OUT OF THE historical traditions which have been allowed to survive in the Pentateuch as a framework for the giving of the law a fairly straightforward story emerges. It is summarized as follows by von Rad:

> God, the creator of the world, called the patriarchs and promised them the land of Canaan. When Israel became numerous in Egypt, God led the people through the wilderness with wonderful demonstrations of grace; then after their lengthy wandering he gave them under Joshua the Promised Land.[1]

T. J. Meek, in his *Hebrew Origins,* expands this somewhat as follows:

> The first Hebrew was Abram (also called Abraham), who migrated from Ur of the Chaldees to Harran, and from there by command of God to the promised land of Canaan. After a brief sojourn in Egypt he and his family settled at Hebron in southern Canaan and lived there on friendly terms with the natives. There the family grew and prospered, remaining aloof from the resident population and marrying only among themselves or with their kinsmen in Harran. In the days of Jacob, however, there came a famine in the land, and learning of the high estate to which his son Joseph had risen in Egypt . . . Jacob was moved to migrate thither with all his family. Here the newcomers were made so welcome and found conditions so propitious that they grew to be a considerable people. Presently, however . . . the Hebrews were compelled to do forced labour for the Egyptians and were reduced to virtual servitude, until a deliverer arose in

---

[1] *Genesis,* S.C.M. Press, London, 1961, pp. 13–14. Note that von Rad speaks of the Hexateuch by inclusion of Joshua rather than of the Pentateuch.

the person of Moses who was commissioned by God to lead his people back to the Promised Land. On the way, God gave the people through Moses at Sinai the laws that were to guide them in their future state. Moses, however . . . died in Moab so that the actual conquest was under the leadership of Joshua. That conquest was immediate and complete. The Canaanites were exterminated and the land was divided by lot among the several tribes. The people now had a land of their own and in due time they demanded and received a king in the person of Saul. Out of small beginnings under the guidance of God a new nation was born, a unique nation, the chosen of God to make him known to the world.[2]

Is this what actually happened? To what extent does this correspond to sober historical fact in so far as the course of events can be reconstructed? I suggest that before going on we give a minute or two to considering to what extent Israel was an ethnic or political unity since this historical question has an important bearing on the theology of community elaborated at a later stage.

Abraham is the first in the Bible to be called a *Hebrew* and this is not an ethnic designation, as the Greek translator correctly saw who rendered it by *ho peratēs*, "the nomad, he who crosses over (from one pasture to another)". The eponymous ancestor of the Hebrews is Eber as mentioned in Genesis 10, the so-called Table of the Nations. *Eber* is linguistically identical with *abiru*, the name in the cuneiform inscriptions for a group which was not an ethnic unity but was made up of marauders, plunderers, nomads, without any fixed political allegiance. This agrees with the Old Testament evidence in that the term Hebrew is never used there by a Hebrew of himself, but seems to be "a degrading, derogatory appellation, a mark of inferiority denoting an alien, a barbarian, a Bedouin . . . a mock-name that ridicules its bearers"[3] – rather like the original sense of *christian*. It is now generally agreed that the biblical Hebrews were in some way connected with and probably in origin a part of this heterogeneous social mass, without roots, unattached to the divine reality of the state as conceived at that time. Israel, at any rate, came into existence

[2] Harper Torchbook, New York, pp. 1–2.
[3] Rabbi Parzen, quoted in Meek, *op. cit.*, p. 10.

amid a welter of races and race movements. They were pre-dominantly but not exclusively semitic. Many of the social customs of patriarchal times, land-tenure, levirate marriage, for example, appear to have been originally non-semitic. We cannot even be absolutely certain that Abraham was a semite despite his name. Jacob appears in the old cultic prayer in Deuteronomy 26 as the "wandering Aramaean". Ezekiel reminds Jerusalem that "your father was an Amorite and your mother a Hittite" (16.3).

This fits in with the biblical story at many points. The first patriarchs are aliens in Palestine – they do not belong in the society of that time which was already deeply entrenched there. Their situation in Egypt was that familiar to the *apiru* for centuries all over the Near East, and the legislator reminds their kinsmen of a later day, "You have experienced what it means to be an alien" (Ex. 23.9). We find people of non-Israelite stock entering the covenant at different times – the men of Gibeon, for example (Jos. 9). Moreover, as all now admit, not all the Hebrews went down into Egypt and not all of those who did so came out at the same time. The fusion out of which the tribal union was born took much longer than one might suspect from a first reading of the texts.

This means that far from the term *Israel* signifying a political reality, a state, it referred in the first place to the collectivity of those who had renounced their political allegiance, who chose for one reason or another to stay outside of the all-enclosing divine reality of the state with its tutelary deities. The choice of the supernatural overlord Yahweh was a means of expressing this and, more important, the means for creating a unity of a different kind. In prophetic thinking Israel is never identical with the political structure, the monarchic state which came into existence about a century and a half after the settlement. On the contrary, the monarchy and monarchic state meet with almost unqualified disapproval in prophetic writing. Israel existed before the state; it continued to exist after the state as such disappeared. We must therefore look elsewhere if we wish to find a principle of unity and solidarity.

The most obvious thing in the records is that Israel was

originally a community born out of an intolerable situation. It was also an open-ended society in that others could and did become part of it on condition of entering the covenant, that is, of accepting as relevant for themselves the exodus-event. So the Gibeonites ask to enter the covenant but only after they say – or are made to say by the editor – that they had heard a report about Yahweh and all that he had done in Egypt (Jos. 9.9). It is therefore no exaggeration to say, as Mendenhall does, that "early Israel was an ecumenical faith, a Catholic religion in the best sense of the term, the very purpose of which was to create a unity among a divided and warring humanity".[4]

Though it is a far haul from these early days to New Testament times, this could already give the perceptive some insight into what kind of a community the Church is meant to be. We shall come to this more directly in a moment. It will be obvious that any group coming together under the circumstances described above will take some time to articulate its consciousness of its own identity. In other words, the theologies of community (if this is not too pretentious a term) or community-models which we find in the Pentateuch are the product of reflection some time after the events. There are, broadly speaking, two of these: that which can be reconstructed from the Northern or Elohist strand taken up by the Deuteronomists; the other in the Priestly document. The Yahwist must be considered apart, since he is more concerned with what we may call sapiential questions – the factors causing disintegration in human society in particular.

The Northern or Elohist tradition is centrally important here since it is the bearer of the covenant idea which is taken up later in Deuteronomy. It has been profoundly influenced by the great prophets of the North in the ninth (Elijah, Elisha) and eighth (Amos, Hosea) centuries. In order, therefore, to see a consistent community-model emerging one would have to study the Elohist, Deuteronomy and the prophets referred to.

We can take one aspect of this community thinking as an example of the continuity within this tradition. In an Elohist passage in Exodus 18 we find Moses dispensing justice to the

[4] In *Biblical Archaeologist*, 25 (1962), 73–74.

community in the desert. The community is divided into 1,000s, 100s and 10s, we might say into dioceses and parishes. Finding that he was no longer able to cope, he gets some good advice from his father-in-law who suggests that he subdelegate his authority: "Choose able men from all the people . . . men who are trustworthy and hate a bribe and place such men over the people" (Ex. 18.21). Moses acts on this and these men become responsible for the ordinary administration of justice, though there was some machinery for passing on the more difficult cases to Moses himself as the charismatic leader. The same incident reappears in the first chapter of Deuteronomy but here we are told that *the people* chose their own representatives who were then *appointed* by Moses. So here we have representation and authorization together. In Numbers 11, also from the Northern tradition, Moses is told by Yahweh to appoint seventy men of the people. These were placed around the tent "and the Lord took some of the spirit that was upon him (Moses) and put it upon the seventy elders; and when the spirit rested upon them they prophesied" (Num. 11.25). At this point comes the awkward and unpredictable element, usually so embarrassing for those in authority. There were two men in the camp who were "prophesying" although they had not been "ordained" and Joshua, speaking for all institutions which fear the unpredictable, asked Moses to silence them. "But Moses said to him: 'Are you jealous for my sake? Would that all the Lord's people were prophets that the Lord would put his spirit upon them!' " (11.29). We are reminded here not only of the exorcists whom Jesus refused to silence but of the at times disconcerting function of prophets in the early Church who were held in higher honour than administrators and could even preside over the Eucharist.

The charismatic principle, vital for this idea of community, operates not only in the appointment of leaders but also in succession to office. The succession of Joshua to Moses gives the clearest example of this. We find Moses asking, in Numbers 27.16: "Let Yahweh, the God of the spirits of all flesh, appoint a man over the congregation . . . that the congregation of Yahweh may not be as sheep which have no shepherd", and Yahweh replies, "Take Joshua son of Nun, *a man in whom is the spirit,* and lay your hand upon him." This also is taken up in Deuteronomy where we read that "Joshua son of Nun was full of the spirit of wisdom, for Moses had laid his hands upon him" (34.9). In view of what is to follow, we may add that this incident, as recorded in Numbers, has been re-edited by post-exilic priestly circles who insist that Eleazar the priest had a hand in the appointment. We find a purer form of this charismatic succession to office in the succession of Elisha, the disciple of Elijah. He prays for a double share of his master's spirit (a double share is that due to the eldest son according to the law of primogeniture) which is promised him on condition that he sees Elijah as he is being taken up. He does so and is invested with the prestigious mantle of the holy man with which he works miracles. We will see later that this scene must have been in Luke's mind in describing the ascension of Jesus: the disciples looking up, the being clothed with power from on high, the coming of the spirit on the prophetic community, the miraculous exercise of the charismatic gifts, including prophecy, which is attributed to the Spirit of Jesus.

What is the link between the historical Israel of the earliest period, the community welded together by communal sharing of an intolerable situation, and the theological ideal which we have sketched here? It is surely the consciousness of being a society formed by free association. This term is not used in the liberal democratic sense according to which the function of society is simply to create the optimum conditions for the individual to develop and enrich his personality (and make money, considered as an extension of personality). It expressed not only the common sharing of an interpretation of the founding event, the Escape, but also a mutual commitment which determined the kind of common life which was to be lived. Freedom was established in principle by breaking away from the theological determinism of myth; but it still had to be achieved in the common life under the covenant. It certainly meant that Israel was not *a system;* and this reflected directly upon the character and exercise of office in the community.

What is above all emphasized in this tradition is that the community lives by a principle which is not identical with its own structure. It lives by *grace,* the divine election expressed in the exodus-event. It lives by *tradition* in the sense of attachment to and re-actualization of a primal experience. It lives by *the spirit* which gives life to the structure and without which all aspects of institutional life are dead. Another characteristic of this prophetic tradition is that it takes the desert generation as the ideal Israel. Then Israel lived from day to day and did not run the risk of identifying itself with a political structure. This means that they thought of Israel as a pilgrim-church working out a destiny in its march through history. It means also that Israel must refuse to absolutize and thus become enslaved to religious symbols. Amos makes this point clearly: "Did you bring to me sacrifices and offerings the forty years in the wilderness, O house of Israel?" (5.25), but it is present throughout the prophetic writings. It must not absolutize either the exodus-tradition (Amos 9.7) or the covenant idea (Ps. 10.16) or, above all, the temple (Jer. 7) or, much less, any of its institutions or offices, including the monarchy.

The continuity between this ancient community-model and the Christian Church could be established by a study of the relevant material in the New Testament but it would take us beyond the scope of this essay. It is established on the linguistic level by the fact that the *qahal* of Deuteronomy incorporates this ancient tradition and is translated in the Greek by *ekklesia* which is the starting-point for the use of this term in the New Testament. This term, being liturgical, directs our attention to the local eucharistic community in which, to use Rahner's phrase, the Church becomes event.

There is one other remark to be made about the community thinking behind this book. We can detect here, despite the exalted community theology and the insistence on divine election – the basis of our Christian doctrine of grace – the germs of that exclusivism and triumphalism which were to undermine the canonical community-idea in the post-exilic period. There are several indications of this but three might serve as examples:

1. It contains an elaborate Holy-war ideology, projected back

to the time of the Settlement, but an expression of a nationalism and religious fanaticism which did not bode well for the future.

2. "Neighbour" is identical in this book with "fellow Israelite". Compare the answer of Jesus to the question of the scribe and the parable which followed. This kind of racialism was directly contrary to the original idea of Israel as an inter-racial and open society.

3. It contains restrictive legislation debarring certain classes from the liturgical assembly (chapter 23), including the maimed, eunuchs, the illegitimate and, again, those of mixed blood.

Interesting to note that the Qumran community adopted and intensified these regulations in its Community Rule, with which we can contrast the words of Jesus on the classes of people who would enter the Kingdom of God – even in advance of the moral theologians of that time.

The other community-model represented in the Pentateuch is that which can be inferred from what is generally known, for want of a better name, as the Priestly document. Before going on to discuss this, two misconceptions have to be cleared away if we are not to falsify the picture by over-simplification.

The first is that, as far as we know, the "priestly" element was present in Israel from early times and in fact finds its place in the community-model discussed above. If we accept some form of the amphictyony hypothesis for the political organization of early Israel in Canaan this will be especially apparent since an amphictyony demands a central sanctuary and this needs priests at least as cult-functionaries. We should remember, moreover, that the crucial phrase about Israel being "a kingdom of priests, a holy nation" is found in an Elohist passage (Ex. 19.6) and seems to be genuinely ancient. The Deuteronomic community also has room for priests ("levitical priests" as they are invariably called in this book) who are not just cult-functionaries but have a judicial function as well. The levites have a special importance for Deuteronomy as a whole since it seems that they were the traditioners of the ancient cultic material found here and the creators of the homiletic style which is used to express so many of the concepts – grace, election, listening to the Word of God – necessary for the life of the community. Thus we cannot speak without qualification of an early priestless model and a late priestly one.

Secondly, it is not self-evident that the prophetic polemic against priesthood, clearly felt in the prophetic editing of the story of Samuel at Shiloh and in the eighth-century prophets, is against the office as such rather than against the corruption of worship at the local shrines. Some of the prophets had themselves a connection with cult and one or two of them were priests (conspicuously, Jeremiah). Besides, the priestly editors of a later age did not delete those passages condemning contemporary religious practices and the corrupt priesthoods which sponsored them, which we would have expected them to if they had understood them in this absolute sense. Thus we cannot speak without qualification of an absolute opposition between prophet and priest, prophetic community and priestly community.

At the same time, the predominance of the priestly caste in the post-exilic period, which is reflected in various ways in the editing of ancient tradition in the Pentateuch, in effect deeply modified the community-pattern and structure discernible in the earlier sources.

The final all-inclusive priestly opus goes from creation (Gen. 1) to Exile. It can be fairly easily recognized – wherever you have genealogies, complex time-divisions, detailed cultic enactments, its presence may be suspected. The covenant is still basic – in fact the history of humanity is now punctuated by a series of covenants going back to Noah. Even in the desert period the community is seen as liturgical with functions precisely allotted and circumscribed. Not unnaturally, we find priests playing a considerable role in community affairs. We have seen the case of Eleazar in the "ordination" of Joshua. Another example would be the battle of wits with the Egyptian magicians in which, in the priestly edition, Aaron has his part to play. How was the community-idea affected in practice?

Perhaps the ultimate explanation, behind all the at times rather unpleasant phenomena that we meet with in the priestly writings, is the concept of God found there. A good test case is the rebellion of Korah, which ends with the rebel being swallowed up by a precisely engineered earthquake. One imagines that the two unauthorized prophets whom Moses refused to silence would have received short shrift from the sacerdotal god. There is also the swift and spectacular retribution visited on Nadab and Abihu for committing a purely ritual irregularity – using the wrong kind of incense (Lev. 10). There is a strong element of the unpredictable and even demonic in the priestly god which would perforce undermine the confidence of those who are bound to him in covenant or at least lead to a slavish sort of service. Fear and not love is the predominant emotion in this area of Old Testament religion.

Besides this, the very presence of an hereditary priesthood, growing all the time in numbers and influence and exercising an increasing power over the community, was fatal to the old canonical idea. It created a class-distinction unknown in the earlier period between cleric and lay (the latter word occurs for the first time in the Priestly document) which was to lead to the condition castigated by Jesus in the New Testament. As between the priestly and learned on one side and the *am ha-haretz*, the profane laity, on the other, there is no doubt where his sympathies lay.

Where does all this lead to? The New Testament Church is described as "God's own people", "the Israel of God", "the people of the covenant" and similar terms, all of which are intended to show that the Christian Church fulfils the community of Israel. The community-ideal or community-model was not thought up by Jesus or anyone else as a brand-new blueprint or imported from outside the area in which all their thinking was carried out, namely, the Scriptures which they heard read in the service and by which they lived. Hence the relevance of community-models in the Old Testament. The Church fulfils Israel, but which Israel? Where in the Scriptures is the ideal taken up by Jesus and the apostles and projected into the future? Despite the Constitution on the Church of Vatican II we are still trying to answer that question.

X

Can we Pray the Cursing
Psalms?

ONE OF THE MOST surprising things for the Christian who has
been brought up to think of the Bible – all of it – as the living
oracles of God is to find in the Book of Psalms expressions of the
most fiercely uncompromising hate for one's fellow men side by side
with songs of praise and rapt adoration of God. Take Psalm 109.
It starts with an invocation addressed to God by someone who is
evidently in bad trouble and who goes on at once to pray *against*
an unnamed enemy. He wants all kinds of horrible things to
happen to him including unemployment (and there was no
National Assistance then) and bankruptcy. He prays:

> May his days be few,
> may another seize his goods!
> May his children be fatherless,
> and his wife a widow!
> May his children wander about and beg,
> may they be driven out of the ruins they inhabit!

– and so on, until he sums it all up, when he comes out of breath to
the end of the litany, in one compendious curse:

> He clothed himself with cursing as his coat,
> may it soak into his body like water,
> like oil into his bones!

This is exceptionally strong meat, but we find the same kind
of language throughout the whole collection. So, to take another
example, in that beautiful hymn sung by the exiles beside the
Babylonian waters (Ps. 137) there comes at the end, right out of
the blue, a blessing pronounced on the one who should dash

out the brains of the children of the common enemy against the nearest rock!

Now unless we are completely beyond being shocked even by the Bible we are bound to ask: can this be inspired by God? And if so, what kind of a God is it that finds this sort of prayer acceptable? Can we seriously be expected to *pray* this? After all, the psalms, which were the Hymns Ancient and Modern of the temple, were used by Christ and the early Christians, and in fact the psalm with which we began was quoted in the first Christian liturgical assembly (Acts 1.20). They are used constantly in the liturgy and prayed day and night by priests, monks and others who recite the divine office. Perhaps that is why the Church has always insisted until recently on the use of Latin!

Seriously, though, what are we to make of these psalms? One answer, already adopted by some Christian bodies, is quietly to drop them. If we do this, however, we find ourselves with two problems on our hands, one practical the other theoretical. The practical problem is to know how much to drop since, as C. S. Lewis said, the cursing parts do not "come away clean" and there are other psalms, not of the cursing type, which we might want to drop also. A good example would be Psalm 68 which not even the scholars can do much with and which W. F. Albright thinks is made up of a disconnected list of song-headings from ancient times. The theoretical problem is, of course, to understand why they are there at all, how they can be Word of God. A great many attempts have been made to answer this problem, some of them more ingenious than convincing. St Thomas came back to it on more than one occasion. His two chief arguments are: that the sentiments expressed in these psalms are directed against the sin as distinct from the sinner and/or that they deal with what the psalmist foresees *will* happen, not what he *wants* to happen. Not all have found these arguments convincing. The first seems to be questionable on the grounds of sound psychology as the second certainly is on those of grammar. In more recent times, others have argued that these strong expressions were intended providentially as an antidote to a permissive and tepid age like our own, and they go on to remind us that the anger is in fact a *theological* anger, that the psalmist is expressing the divine anger:

> Do I not hate them that hate thee, O Lord?
> Do I not loathe them that rise up against thee?
> I hate them with a perfect hatred! (Ps. 139.21–22)

But what a dangerous game this is! Perhaps weakest of all is the appeal which one often hears to an Oriental habit of exaggerating to get heightened effect. It is extremely doubtful whether anyone has ever proved that Orientals are more prone to exaggeration than Occidentals or, for that matter, Eskimos or Bushmen.

It seems to me that we can best approach the problem by recalling that the curse was first and foremost a solemn juridical formula considered as legally binding and supported by the sanction of God upon whose will the whole social order rested. In the absence of a police force and of any effective machinery for bringing the evildoer to justice – and this applied also to international relations – the only way open for obtaining the minimum of justice without which life was not worth living was the kind of sanction involved in the curse. This at least was taken seriously. Anyone who has lived in a country where law-enforcement is either non-existent or ineffective will have no difficulty in imagining what this means. What runs through these psalms even at their crudest, as through the at times equally disconcerting words of the prophets, is the burning need for justice.

Let us recall too that these people had no clear idea of a future life where, as the Christian believes, justice is not only done but seen to be done, where the respective roles of the Rich Man and Lazarus are reversed. That God's hand should be seen here where gross injustice seemed to go unobserved and unpunished was the condition of their faith itself. The very existence of God was at stake.

This means that these imprecations were, in fact, for the poor man fighting his battle for faith in an almost total darkness, a prayer for God to show his hand, vindicate the social order which was part of his own divine order and bring redress. And before we dismiss this too rapidly let us also recall that the curse pronounced by Jesus as judge is concerned exclusively with justice within human society. It was pronounced on those who do not feed the hungry or clothe the naked or look after the sick and the deprived (Mt. 25.41-45).

The curse, then, was essentially a juridical formula. It was never pronounced in an arbitrary or capricious way, but when once pronounced was considered absolutely binding and efficacious. It was used as a form of excommunication, a means of dissociating oneself from an individual guilty of gravely sinful (that is, anti-social) conduct until such time as he decided to repent. In the ceremony of covenant-renewal the whole community freely took upon itself quite a repellent list of curses (they can be found in Dt. 28). They really believed these curses would come on them if they broke the covenant. In so doing they were not foolishly enslaving themselves; they were expressing in the most extreme terms known to them the manner of their commitment and the risk involved in this kind of decision.

There is a further case, perhaps more to our immediate purpose. A curse was self-administered in a trial especially in the rare case of trial by ordeal – rather like our swearing on the Bible. In Numbers 5 we find an excerpt from a Jewish ritual laying down the correct procedure in the case of a woman suspected of marital infidelity. It hardly makes pleasant reading but at least it served the purpose of giving her a chance to clear her good name. She was given holy water mixed with dust from the sanctuary floor to drink and at the same time freely accepted the consequences of the curse pronounced over her by the priest: "May this water which brings the curse pass into your body and make it swell" – knowing that, if she was innocent, she had nothing to fear. It may be, as some have supposed, that in Psalm 109 the afflicted victim of injustice is simply quoting the imprecations made against him during a trial at which he had been falsely accused of some grave crime. He tells God of what they wanted to happen to him since he knows, in his near despair, that only God can break through the web of evil which is closing round him, though innocent, and which he can already feel in his bones.

Having said all this, however, we might still doubt the wisdom of recommending the general use of these psalms even if our age is permissive and tepid – on which not all are agreed. We know how these psalms have been used to justify all sorts of persecutions and oppression in the name of religion and a righteous (sometimes self-righteous) God and of a militant Christian faith before which all human rights could be safely relativized. We Catholics are fortunately no longer so sure that God is on our side *against* others, we no longer have much use for the *anathemata* of past councils and are trying, at times with touching urgency, to get rid of a congenital war psychology and total self-assurance in religious matters. There is also the fact that, at a deeper and more personal level, our complexes are liable, if we are not careful, to be worked off on other people. Maybe the religious attitudes we have been talking about explain why, in a progressive society which is trying increasingly to apply remedial treatment to the criminal, the Catholic is often precisely the one who insists on punishment, on what used to be called vindictive justice. In view of all this, it would be a tragedy if psalms like these were to provide such people with the wrong kind of ammunition.

One final point. These almost animal cries from the depths are part of a whole movement, a forward line which ends in the mystery of the Cross. Even within the Old Testament, we find that as time goes on intercession for the evildoer tends more and more to take the place of this primitive and harsh cry for justice, culminating in that mysterious figure of the Servant who "bore the sins of many and made intercession for sinners" (Is. 53.12). This looks forward to the point where, as Simone Weil put it, the world of necessity meets the world of perfect justice, and for the Christian there can be no solution apart from the all-forgiving figure on the Cross.

XI

The Impasse of Death in the Old Testament

THE FIRST TASK of every religion is to provide an answer, an oracle, in the face of death. Christianity, once identified as a religion, could hardly be exempted from performing this task, and in fact did provide its own answer in the framework of the scriptural contemplation of death, but with reference to the entirely new experience of the death of Christ. Death is never seen as a purely neutral event, something which happens to a man. It is intensely moral and personal, following on man's failure to realize his own being as a spiritual and moral possibility – expressed telegrammatically in Paul's saying about death coming into the world through sin (Rom. 5.12). This failure is overcome only in the perfect obedience of Jesus expressed in the positive acceptance or appropriation of death, even death on the cross. There is therefore for the Christian no philosophy of death but only the action of Jesus which breaks the impasse and is crowned by resurrection. The answer lies here and here only. But the way in which this answer is framed by the New Testament takes us back to how the question was asked in the first place and therefore to the existential situation, the terror or revulsion or agony, from which the death of Christ is contemplated. This can be illustrated in the way that Paul, in proclaiming to the Christians of Corinth the mystery of the final resurrection, quotes from one of those Isaian oracles in which breathes the hope of the reborn community after the Exile:

Death is swallowed up in victory! (1 Cor. 15.54).

He will swallow up death for ever, and the Lord God will wipe away tears from all faces, and the reproach of his people he will take away from the earth; for the Lord has spoken (Is. 25.8).

Behind this expression about death being swallowed up there lies the old mythological idea of the death of Mot (that is, Death), lord of the underworld and its denizens. It is inferred that so long as the disastrous alien force of death is at work in life which is the property of God the victory of God cannot be complete and final.

In the annals of the early monarchy and those vivid stories in Judges, many of them originally of purely secular interest, there is an attitude to death which is immediate and naïve rather than theological and reflective. It has much in common with the attitude found in the Homeric poems which, it has been claimed, are dominated by the polar ideas of divinity and death. According to this "heroic" view of death, it is above all necessary to avoid dying "as a fool dies" (2 Sam. 3.33) – by accident, or stupidly walking into a trap, or by the hand of a woman. Better to die by one's own hand than run this risk, as seen in the case of Abimelek wounded before the city of Thebez. Heroic death is always public and catastrophic, and since it is by preference sudden and in the heat of battle neither requires nor allows for any special preparation. Even David, who dies in his bed, does so giving instructions for the liquidation of a surviving enemy with no thought for the memorable phrase or the deathbed oracle, or, much less, for preparing to meet his Maker. In this scene we are very far from the Christian ideal of the *bona mors*.

Reflection came only at a later stage. According to the Creation prologue (Gen. 1) man is given the breath of life by God and is made in the image of God. This challenges the contemporary pagan idea that man was a mere puppet created uniquely to take care of the shrines of the gods and carry their statues in procession. But Genesis agrees with the ancient cosmogonies in denying to man autonomous existence. The only difference is that, for these latter, evil and death are built into man and therefore present from the first moment of his existence. In the old Babylonian story of Gilgamesh the ale-wife Siduri speaks for all antiquity when she says to the hero:

G

Gilgamesh, where are you wandering?
The life you are seeking you will not find.
When the gods created mankind
death for mankind they allotted,
life in their own hands retaining.

In the biblical view, on the contrary, death had no part in the divine plan but entered from outside, as the result of failure or sin, and thus got a foothold. The story of Adam and Eve lays down and illustrates the spiritual law that sin involves diminution and eventually extinction of life. So the original generous life-span (the pre-Flood patriarchs beginning with Adam) is gradually reduced in the measure that sin extends its hold and widens its bridgehead until we come to the total, or almost total, extinction of the Flood.

This process continues after the Flood, but with God's call to Abraham the process is reversed, the ebb-tide turns to flow. What God promises through Abraham is *beraka*, blessing, happiness and fullness of life. This did not involve, for those conscious of receiving this blessing, a life after death which would have provided a simple answer to the impasse. Strange though it may seem to us, their association with God did not involve for them the thought of life with God after death. Death remains for Old Testament man in general something dark and wholly undesirable. There is here little of the intuition which we find in some Egyptian texts of a luminous existence beyond the tomb. To die is to go down into Sheol, the underworld, which is the home of the shades, those who continue in a diminished and bloodless existence. When Jacob is shown the bloodied garment of his son he cries out: "In mourning I shall go down to Sheol, to my son . . ." There is no halo round the head of Samuel when he comes up from Sheol at the bidding of the woman of Endor.

What is paradoxical in this view of death is that it was regarded as undesirable chiefly because it seemed to be a severance from God. The *nephesh*, the living person of blood and breath, has a direct existential relationship with God not only through creation and the spirit which is breathed into him but also through the life of worship for which he is created. It is no coincidence that the first Creation account or recital is clearly a liturgical document. Once dead, he would no longer be able to go to Jerusalem and the temple and take part in the joyful liturgies of the great pilgrim feasts, he would no longer "see the Face", meet God on his own ground, around the altar of sacrifices:

> Thou hast said: "Seek ye my face",
> My heart says to thee: "Thy face, Lord, I do seek".
> Hide not thy face from me! (Ps. 27.8–9)

It was the temple which was the abode of the Presence, the Face; it was there that the living met and entered into a close and joyful communion with the God who gives life. The divine worship of the temple, more than anything else, gave Old Testament man the sense of the divine presence, the feeling for the hidden dimension of human existence, what communion in the will and the life of God could mean. All this seemed to end with death:

> In death there is no remembrance of thee;
> in the underworld who can give thee praise? (Ps. 6.5)

> Sheal cannot thank thee,
> death cannot praise thee;
> those who go down to the pit cannot hope for thy
>   faithfulness. (Is. 38.18)

The paradox therefore lies in the fact that the horror of death which permeates reflection and prayer in so many of the psalms is not just the natural revulsion which all feel – the *timor mortis conturbat me* of the medieval poet – but is above all theological. It goes with fear of being severed from the life of union with God and hidden from his presence. This explains why the psalmist prays to be delivered from the gates (that is, the power) of death (Ps. 9.13), the sleep of death (Ps. 13.3), the dust of death (Ps. 22.15), the valley of the shadow of death (Ps. 23.4), from the pit (Ps. 28.1). From this we can deduce at once something very important, namely, that belief is an existence after death does not emerge as a result of philosophical speculation but along the line of man's here-and-now existence. We have to wait for the Book of Wisdom, written in Greek outside of Palestine a bare half-century before

Christ, for the first more or less philosophical statement about immortality. In the meantime, we see how, from the experience of the divine presence gained through prayer and especially liturgical prayer and action, the Hebrew inferred, gradually but with increasing sureness, that association with God was of such a kind that death could not rub it out. There is some intimation of this in a psalm which was to become an often quoted proof-text for early Christians:

> Therefore my heart is glad, and my soul rejoices;
> my body also dwells secure.
> For thou dost not give me up to Sheol,
> or let thy godly one see the Pit.
> Thou dost show me the path of life;
> in thy presence there is fulness of joy,
> in thy right hand are pleasures for evermore
>   (Ps. 16.9–11).

This does not, of course, mean that death as a hostile invading power at the service of sin is cancelled out or has become insignificant. To enter the underworld means really to enter into the power of death and from that dark condition only God can rescue, since only in him is the source and origin of life. The Old Testament God is not only "the living god" – he is never represented as a dying and rising god like Baal or Osiris – but the God who gives life:

> The Lord kills and brings to life;
> he brings down to Sheol and raises up (1 Sam. 2.6).

> After two days he will revive us;
> on the third day he will raise us up
> that we may live before him (Hos. 6.2).

The descent of Christ into the underworld, which we profess in the creed, represents the rescuing act of God foreshadowed here and elsewhere in the Old Testament. Christ places himself in the power of death but in so doing he penetrates the kingdom of death and robs it of its power.

The life which is proper to God both for the Old Testament and the pagan world of that time and in which, according to

Hebrew faith, men are called to share, is stronger than death and all the negative forces at work in human existence which culminate in death. The Old Testament speaks of that life in metaphorical and symbolic terms more telling than discursive and philosophical language. It is light in its pure state, it is a fountain of living water springing up everlastingly. The psalmists even suppose that the very desire which they experience of union with God as the source and centre of existence proves the possibility of transcending death just as surely as the very fact that they experience thirst proves the possibility of drinking – that water must exist:

> Thou givest them drink from the river of thy delights.
> For with thee is the fountain of life;
> in thy light do we see light (Ps. 36.8–9).

XII

On Saving One's Soul

The Biblical View of Man as "Soul"

The oldest consistent biblical view of man, that which emerges from the corpus put together probably during the reign of Solomon (the Yahwist work), brings out with a concrete and satisfying amplitude of vision and with compelling images a profound intuition into the ambiguous position which man holds in the hierarchy of nature to which he belongs but which he in part transcends. He has much in common with the animal world, but he is also "just a little lower than the *elohim*". Yahweh God made him out of clay and breathed into his nostrils the breath of life. He thus became "a living soul", *nephesh hayyah*. The word usually translated "soul", *nephesh*, seems to have been primitively connected with breathing, as also the word "spirit", *ruah*. More primitively, the meaning was "neck" or "throat", which provided some difficulty for earlier translators of the Old Testament. In Psalm 69.1, for example, Jerome has "the waters have come into my soul" whereas the more correct translation is, "the waters have come up to my neck".

What makes man "a soul" is his origin in the divine activity. When he dies this mysterious God-given energy recedes with his breath, going out of him through his throat and nostrils to return to its source. "As her life went out of her", we read of Rachel, "she called his name 'Son of my Sorrow' ". There is no question of the separation of soul and body. Man ceases at death to be "a soul" and becomes a corpse. There is no word in Hebrew for body apart from a dead body. In the light of this, it is easy to see how misleading the translation-word "soul" could be since it brings to the mind something very different from what was in the mind of the original writer. But before going on to see how this confusion of anthropologies happened, it would be useful to get a clear idea of what the Old Testament really says on this subject.

In the Old Testament man is not a soul in a body in the Platonic and Neo-platonic sense of a prisoner in a prison or a sailor in a ship. The body–soul polarization is not supposed except in the obvious sense that bodily structure and function do not exhaust man's idea of his personality. The difference has to be traced back to the manner of perception from which the anthropology proceeds. The perception of Old Testament man was directed above all to a grasped totality; it was also intensely subjective and heightened by an emotional commitment of the subject to an extent difficult for us to imagine today. This was *their* way of knowing. Thus in Exodus 23.9 instead of translating literally as R.S.V. does, "you know the heart of a stranger", we should translate, "you have experienced what it means to be an alien". This explains why in Hebrew there is only verb "to know" which covers a whole range of meaning: getting to know a person, recognition, skill, sexual relations and experience in general. "Soul", therefore, does not necessarily mean the same in scriptural texts as it does in the common acceptance today, and that acceptance has been determined to a large extent by translations of the Scriptures. So very often when the Vulgate has *anima* we should read *persona* and think "subject". An example would be the often misused words of the king of Sodom to Abraham (Ged. 14.21): *da mihi animas caelera tolle*" (Vulgate), which should be translated with R.S.V., "Give me the persons but take the goods for yourself". We shall see in a moment how this bears on the question of saving one's soul.

Rather than as the Platonic *psyche* or the scholastic *forma substantialis*, "soul" in this earliest literary corpus and elsewhere in the Scriptures should be thought of as the centre of consciousness and subjectivity. Where Jacob, in the Douay version, asks for food "that my soul may bless thee", R.S.V. has simply and correctly, "that I may bless thee before I die". Again, in the story of the rape of Dinah, after the momentary outburst of passion we are told that Shechem's soul adhered to her, by which we are to understand that what began as lust ended in a genuine emotional and personal commitment. Thus also "the soul" of Jonathan clave to that of David and he loved him "as his own soul". There is a wealth of emotive meaning in these phrases that we can easily miss. "The soul" is the inner core of self-awareness, with all that comes from it, which gives cohesion and power to a man's personality and which a false approach to "the spiritual life" can do so much to disintegrate. But we are anticipating.

In the historical books we have the same usage. The *nephesh* is the root of the vital energy and dynamism of a man and its divine origin is never lost sight of. Over all this turbulent, brutal, often moving world of treachery, vendetta and occasional heroism there stands as a basic postulate the sacrality of this vital centre of man's life. It is to God that life belongs and who protects "the soul" of his own. "The soul of my lord", says Abigail to David, "is bound up in the bundle of life before Yahweh your God" (1 Sam. 25.29). Elijah, in a fit of depression, asks God to *take back* his soul. King Zedekiah swears to Jeremiah, "by the living lord who has made us this soul". Here we can see that the ideas of "soul" and "life" are correlative. An important deduction from this is that these two undergo a progressive deepening of meaning within the revelational process resulting from a continual deepening of religious experience. It is often overlooked that progress comes about not so much through the discovery of new truths, such as personal immortality, as through human experience itself, part of which lies in an increasingly intensified and purified dialogue between the subject and God. A clear test-case of this is the attitude taken up before the fearful prospect of death and the consequent prospect of the disintegration of personality for people who had no clearly-defined ideas on a future life. We see elsewhere how no prayer crops up so often in the psalms as that for deliverance from death and not just because all find, as Agag did, that death is indeed bitter, but paradoxically because it was seen as a severance from life with God especially in the shared liturgical life of the community. Hezekiah's prayer,

spoken at the the point of death, is a moving testimony to this
(see Is. 38.9–20).

This might at first sight seem to block further progress, but
that is not what happened. It meant that the breakthrough, when
it came, was not effected by inventing another life different from
this, a "happy land far, far away", but by having to discover in
and through experience what the real dimensions of this here-
and-now life of union with God and the community meant. This
is a point which has to be borne constantly in mind in reading and
praying the psalms. The difficulty for us in really getting the
point is that our thinking has been so deeply if unconsciously
influenced by Platonic and Cartesian dualism. It is so natural for
us to accept as an orthodox Christian point of view the Myth of
Er at the end of Plato's *Republic* in which the soul, imprisoned in
the body, is represented as the inmate of a dark cave trying to
make his way painfully and slowly to the point of light at the
end of the cave. So, for example, when the psalmist utters his
assurance:

> You will not abandon my soul to Sheol,
> or let thy godly one see the Pit (Ps. 16)

there is no question of the resurrection of the body as we now
understand it. The mention of the heart, the body, the flesh, the
soul, is all part of an attempt to express the totality of the conscious, sentient organism that man is. It is this which must pass
in its entirety through the gates of death to a deeper and richer
experience of the divine presence. Something of this comes through
also in the great Psalm 22 which has left such an impression on
the evangelical passion-story. "My soul will live to him", the
psalmist cries out in defiance, "despite those who go down to the
dust." The self-realization and self-actualization which prayer
begets results in a continual dialogue: "*my soul* pants after thee,
O my God . . . *my soul* thirsts for thee, the living God . . . I pour
out *my soul* to thee . . . why art thou cast down, O *my soul*?"

The Deuteronomists introduce a new formula found in the
shema: "You shall love the Lord your God with all your heart,
with all your soul and with all your strength" (Dt. 6.4). This

again does not invite us to dichotomize or trichotomize the human personality. Soul, heart (that is, mind), strength, are ways of expressing the sum total of vital energy at the disposal of the centre and which ought to go into the searching after and love of God.

In the Priestly writings we find what we might call a standardization of the term "soul". Here it stands quite simply for "human being" and it is no doubt because of this that we use the word vaguely in common parlance, as, for example, "a city of 10,000 souls". There is nothing in the Priestly Creation recital (Gen. 1) about man becoming a "living soul" by means of the divine breath. The distance between this and the earlier Creation account (Gen. 2) can be seen in the fact that *nephesh hayyah*, which means "living person" in the latter, is used only of the animal world below man in the former. Perhaps not enough notice has been taken of the bearing which the dietetic laws in Leviticus 11 have on the Creation recital in the first chapter of Genesis. There is an inner logical and artistic connection between the creation of man on the sixth day and that of the vegetation meant for his nutrition on the third. Later on, in the Noachic covenant, he is permitted also to eat flesh-meat but there are restrictions, and the matter of his provisioning is always surrounded with a kind of penumbra of sacrality due to the great importance of animals in the complex sacrificial system. Man is certainly different from the animal world. He is apart, *holy* (Lev. 11.44), because of his ontological link with God who is the supremely Other. But man has also an intimate link with the animal world, felt intuitively in the Old Testament, expressed more scientifically in the modern epoch. For like man they breathe and bleed, and so flesh which has been strangled or which still has the blood in it is taboo, for "the blood is the life" (Lev. 17.11; Dt. 12.23). The fact that in the course of time the Jewish sacrificial system degenerated into a purely mechanical round of slaughter should not lead us to misconstrue the profound intuition at its starting-point – that the offering of a blood-gift is a sign of the offering of life and of the self.

We would have to go on to show, finally, how the Greek way of looking at man, with its idea of the salvation of the soul *from* the body, enters the Scriptures not only in books written originally in Greek such as the *Wisdom of Solomon* (canonical only for Roman Catholics) but also in the Greek translations of the Hebrew text. We find it everywhere in the intertestamentary literature, for example in the "Address to the Soul" in the Psalms of Solomon. The resultant collisions of rival anthropologies led to tension in every sphere of thought which deals with man and his destiny. The effects of this tension are still with us, perhaps more than we realize. Much of Christian asceticism has been built up on the Greek *psyche–soma* dichotomy. It is well known, to take an outstanding example, how the spiritual life conceived in three progressive stages: *katharsis, elampsis, henosis* (the purgative, illuminative, unitive ways) goes back by direct descent to Neoplatonic thought, and the great medieval mystical tradition stems from the Neo-platonism of Augustine and the writings of Pseudo-Dionysius. This psychological dualism has driven a wedge between consciousness as the core of personality and "soul" as somehow distinct and apart, an object of salvation in its own right. This amounts to a real psychological dislocation which has produced its own concept of Christianity and its own imperatives with regard to secular existence. In keeping with this, the call often heard to "save one's soul" is in many cases not only not scriptural but perhaps not even doctrinally above suspicion.

Save your Life!

One important consequence of all this is that the phrase *salvare animam,* often found in the Vulgate, can be misleading. It is used, for example, in the words of the angel to Lot in the destruction of Sodom, where we ought to translate simply, "Save yourself!" In the mysterious scene of the wrestling at the river Jabbok Jacob exclaims with relief when his anonymous opponent departs, "I have seen God face to face and yet my *life* has been spared!" Here and elsewhere it is a question of physical survival and therefore "life" is required rather than "soul". As we approach the New Testament we find two developments: physical survival is seen as a type of eschatologial survival;

eschatological survival is seen as possible only at the expense of physical survival. In both cases it is a question of preserving one's real identity and integrity in a critical situation. But it is *never* a case of disengaging oneself from the body or matter or the cosmos, the clear proof being that the hope of salvation rests precisely upon the resurrection to a new life in the body, in a reconstituted cosmos, brought about as the result of a great creative act of God.

To look first at physical survival as a type of eschatological survival. In the account of the destruction of Sodom, the angel is certainly intent on securing Lot's physical survival, but in escaping physical death he also escapes judgment. Both are seen on the same plane but in different depth of focus. It was natural enough that this should have been seen by early Christians as a type or figure of the flight of the early community from the doomed city of Jerusalem since the destruction of the city was seen as the crowning judgment on contemporary Judaism and a paradigm of the eschatological judgment (see Mt. 24.15 ff. comparing with Gen. 19.15 ff.). This is quite explicit in Luke's version of the eschatological predictions of Jesus (17.28–33). Interesting to observe further that throughout Old Testament history each turning-point or catastrophe (the terms are identical) is taken as a paradigm showing always more clearly the nature of the goal towards which history is moving. This was especially true of the destruction of Jerusalem in 586 B.C.

It may have been during the time of the Maccabees and the Seleucid persecution that the truth was borne home that real salvation, the preservation of one's full integrity and identity, might be possible only at the price of physical survival. This implied the belief either in some form of personal immortality or in a great re-creative divine act by which the human person would be reconstituted, and it is not a coincidence that the first texts which speak clearly of the resurrection of the dead come from this period of great crisis. Thus Eleazar the martyr suffers in his body (*kata soma*) under the torture but feels joy in his soul (*kata psychen*), and the second of the seven martyr-brothers distinguishes between what he undergoes in the present life and the eternal life which will follow the resurrection. It is clear from the mother's words that her hope is in a new creative act greater than that by which her children were brought into the world. This makes for a decisive doctrinal turning-point in Judaism. We have the working out of a whole theology of crisis and martyrdom, elaborated in part in the context of the hellenistic homily, which was to influence the New Testament. We can summarize by saying that saving one's soul implies action in a critical situation aimed at the survival or reconstitution of the person as such, not of the soul understood in a dualistic sense.

Lose your Life!

The Christian faith implies a crisis of consciousness since the Christian is committed to the view that the final reality, the ultimate self-manifestation of God, is already here in the person of Jesus and compels him to a positive decision. Martyrdom is only the extreme form of this crisis implied in the very fact of being a Christian; the fact that not just theoretically but in bitter earnest the Christian must be prepared at any moment to surrender life and all that goes with it to witness to that final reality. This implies that he can never "sit pretty", be at home in his environment in an absolute sense. Saving one's soul has to be seen in this context rather than in that of an ascetical renunciation of the body. This is what is implied in the crucial gospel-saying:

Whoever would save his life will lose it;
whoever loses his life for my sake and the gospel's will save it
(Mk. 8.35).

If our idea of soul-saving is to be evangelical it must start out from this saying which is one of the best attested in the gospels. The addition of the words "and the gospel's" in Mark reminds us that this gospel was written for a Church then going through its trial by fire and that the saying is consequently a martyrdom-logion addressed to a wider audience than we might at first suppose. As such it receives further emphasis by being placed at the outset of the journey which was to end in the martyrdom of Jesus, a journey which the Christian assembly at Rome gathered together to hear the gospel would see itself repeating. The context in which saving or losing one's life is thought of is clearly not different from that in Maccabees. Only here we are nearer to the Cross and the deepest secret of all which takes us beyond any particular crisis and lights up the whole of existence – namely, that the way to self-realization lies through self-repudiation (for that is, in effect, what denying oneself in the gospel sense means). The same point is made even more forcibly in the form in which the logion is cast in Luke: "whoever tries to *hang on to his life* will lose it, but he who loses his life will preserve it" (17.33).

The same saying is found also in the Fourth Gospel and at the same juncture – the prospect for Jesus of violent death. Here, however, it is universalized in a novel way. Some Greeks had come up to the city for the Passover and asked for an interview with Jesus, approaching for this purpose the disciple with a Greek name, Philip. In answer to an unspecified question, which we may suppose to have been about his death, Jesus states the basic law of Christian existence in terms of the age-old pattern of the death and rebirth of the year and of the grain: "Unless the grain of wheat falls into the ground and dies it remains alone; but if it dies it bears much fruit" (12.24). We may compare this with the *kenosis* hymn in Philippians, the grasping, the holding on, of Adam contrasted with the self-emptying of Jesus the Servant by which he enters into the fullness of life (Phil. 2.5 ff.).

Christianity concerns the Whole Man

One characteristic of our current Christian renewal is the attempt to return upstream to a clearer perception of biblical truth. It is by this that the Church and the individual Christian have to live. Among the forces contriving to distort this truth the earliest, most persistent and deadliest was gnosticism, basically an attempt to restate the gospel in terms of Greek dualism. As an attitude of mind if not as a heresy this is still with us. We have suggested that the call to save one's soul, even when made with the utmost conviction and sincerity, is still too often very much redolent of the gnostic pattern of salvation. We conclude with one or two corollaries stated sketchily more as hints or rough notes for further consideration than anything else:

The Incarnation as the pattern of our "spiritual" life. It is often wrongly suggested that the purpose of Christ's coming into the world was to redeem us from our environment rather than from sin. Note how, for example, in logion 57 of the gnostic Gospel of Thomas, a gospel-saying is twisted into giving a gnostic sense: "He who has known the world has found a corpse . . .". On the contrary, the orthodox view of the Incarnation implies a descent into and transformation of matter; we are to find a divine life, fully humanized, *here, where we are.*

The creation of the whole man. Our mysterious likeness to and kinship with God, stated in the first chapter of the Bible, is basic to the Christian view of man. The old Catechism question, formulated according to the body–soul axis, leaves room for only one answer which though doctrinally unexceptionable is not particularly enlightening. A more biblical view would imply an intuition into that self-awareness, a certain type of self-conscious-ness, which is at the root of identity and personality and which, while differentiating us from the animal world below us, contains a faint reflection of the perfect self-awareness in God expressed through the Word – just as God sees all through his Word so we know and experience through this centre of self-awareness.

The Presence and Operation of Evil. The problem of evil is the starting-point of gnostic speculation. Its equation with matter means that the soul is saved *from* the body. This results in a very different hierarchy of sin from that of orthodox moral teaching. Great prominence is given, in particular, to sexual sin, marital relations are a necessary evil and the *summum bonum* is to cut loose from the world at all costs, as in some suspect forms of early monasticism. In this way evil is vaporized, not faced squarely, even if an intrinsic solution is not at hand, as is the case in the Book of Job.

Human and divine Love. Characteristic of the gnostic view of love is its lack of realism. Human love can never achieve full commit-ment and so the gnostic view feeds on the fiction of a "spiritual" allegiance. On the contrary, the body is the means of union, not separation, because the carnal can and does contain the mystery of the spiritual. The Scriptures do not flinch from representing the divine *agape* in terms of *eros*, as in Hosea, Jeremiah and the Canticle.

Death and after. The gnostic misrepresentation of salvation carries with it the assumption of a complete discontinuity between this world, the only one that we know, and a future world, with the latter usually represented in an unreal, naïve way, really more pagan than Christian. We have seen that the biblical answer to the problem set by death is along the line of a progressive deepening of experience, of what is of serious concern to us here and now. The idea of the soul saved from its here-and-now environment makes us think of our destiny as disembodied spirits – the subject of innumerable bad jokes – rather than the final state of reconstituted personality; a real person in a real world.

XIII

Liturgy and the Incarnation

CONSIDERING THE VOLUME of strictly religious writing which it contains, there is surprisingly little in the Old Testament of the purely personal and mystical. Approach to God was essentially through liturgy as the way in which man in community expressed the totality of his religious experience and aspirations. His liturgical life was not something peripheral, as "going to Mass" is for so many Catholics; it was the way in which he took his place and played his part at the centre of the life of the community which engaged all his potentialities. Liturgy recapitulated all of the religious and social life of man as a member of the community.

But the Old Testament also illustrates how easily liturgy could degenerate into techniques which had to be mastered by specialists and then manipulated for their own interests. This was true of the priesthood and liturgy of Shiloh as described in 1 Samuel 1–3, as also of the cult in the Northern kingdom to judge by the scathing criticism of prophetic figures like Amos and Hosea. It became increasingly true of the post-exilic liturgy, and the widespread rejection of temple-liturgy as a viable form of encounter and religious experience at the time of Christ goes far to explain the at first sight unliturgical character of the New Testament and the gospels in particular.

Yet in spite of this the liturgical ideal remained central in New Testament thinking. It could so remain, however, only at the price of a radical rethinking. In the first place, liturgical language is no longer used in the specialized sense, a language of the sacristy if you wish, but is re-applied to the Christian life in general. For the Christian, the centre is no longer a holy place but a person; Christ is the temple of the new order which contains the divine presence (Jn. 2.21) and the Christian himself is the temple of the Spirit of Christ (Eph. 2.21). St Paul, who cannot be accused of being overliturgical, sees his whole life, his sufferings, his "solicitude for the churches" as a liturgy (*leitourgia*), a worship (*latreia*), a sacrifice (*thusia*), and even in thinking of his death he uses liturgical language – he sees it as the offering of a sacrificial libation: "even if I am to be poured as a libation upon the sacrificial offering of your faith, I am glad and rejoice with you all" (Phil. 2.17), "for I am already on the point of being sacrificed . . ." (2 Tim. 4.6). His labour as missionary and preacher is a spiritual worship of God (Rom. 1.9) and the whole of the physical life of man consecrated to God he sees as "a sacrifice, living, holy and acceptable", a spiritual worship as opposed to the routine of butchery which passes for sacrifice in later Judaism. The basic aim of life, becoming acceptable to God, having access to him, entering the divine presence (Rom. 5.2), is expressed in cultic terms. Nowhere is this clearer than in the First Epistle of Peter:

> Draw near to him; he is the living stone which men rejected but which God has chosen and prized. You too must be built up on him, like living stones, into a spiritual house; you must be a holy priesthood, to offer up that spiritual sacrifice which God accepts through Jesus Christ (2. 4–5).

Here the individual faithful man and woman are seen as taking the place of the temple, now destroyed. They are the new visible symbol of the invisible presence. And in place of the "carnal" sacrificial system of the temple this people must offer the spiritual sacrifice which God can accept through Jesus Christ. It is not at all impossible that the comment of the evangelist on the saying of Jesus about the temple, "but he spoke of the temple of his body" (Jn. 2.21), refers to the community as the Body of Christ in the Pauline sense, the community which has taken the place of the old temple as the liturgical centre.

This community-centredness, so much emphasized today, is however only one aspect of liturgical action. There is also the correlative aspect, less emphasized, of liturgy as the expression of and means towards man's self-realization through incorporation into God by the mediation of the Incarnate Word. This is less emphasized in the Latin Church with its rather more practical and functional approach than the Eastern liturgies, though we might point to the Leonine prayer said at the mixing of wine and water with its key-idea of fellowship in the divine nature (*koinonia*), reminiscent of a well-known passage in 2 Peter (1.4). The action which the *Deus qui humanae substantiae* accompanies has always had the double significance of the participation of man in the divine nature through Christ and the hypostatic union of human nature with the divinity in the person of Christ. In other words, we find here the real theological reason why the Incarnation is central to the liturgy. Its whole purpose is to reveal and create a radically new possibility for our human nature which is actualized in the liturgy. How is this worked out in the Scriptures?

Incarnation is the Latin translation of a Greek word *sarkōsis,* which is not used in the Scriptures but betrays the fact that the doctrine taught in the Church was threshed out during the early centuries with intellectual tools borrowed from the workshop of Greek philosophy. This especially with reference to the key-terms in the long debate, *nature* and *person,* neither of which has a correspondent in Hebrew. It can easily be seen how this kind of philosophical formulation would have been quite impossible in the New Testament milieu. How could the apostles, for example, have thought of Jesus as God, they for whom the only God was Yahweh, "the god of Abraham, Isaac and Jacob", who had glorified his servant and son in the resurrection? (see Acts 3.13). Could Yahweh become man? Unthinkable and blasphemous. A theophany in human guise might have been conceivable for a less sophisticated age (as to Abraham at Mamre in Gen. 18) and in any case such appearances are momentary and present Yahweh incognito. Could a man become Yahweh? Equally unthinkable and blasphemous. Even a term such as "son of God" could only have been thought of at that time in a way such as was common in contemporary Judaism, even though the unique element in the relationship of Jesus to the Father was recognized by those who had lived with him. The very idea of Yahweh begetting in the manner of progenitor-gods such as El, whose son was Baal, would have been abhorrent and practically unthinkable.

We cannot therefore suppose that the earliest Christians claimed divinity in an unspecified way for Jesus and then adduced miracles, prophecy and the rest in support of this claim – much as is found in the older textbooks of apologetics. What we have to explain is how the apostles came to see and acknowledge his real identity and formulate it in the only terms they knew, those of the Jewish faith in which they had been born and bred. It is therefore not surprising that the earliest formulations (if we may use this term) speak neither of the deification of a man or the descent of God but rather of a point where the human meets the divine. The presentation is dynamic rather than conceptual, and is above all scriptural. This means that we will be able to study the most primitive "theology" of the Incarnation in the New Testament only after surveying the *praeparatio evangelica* for the Incarnation in the Old Testament. Here only the briefest outline can be given.

The question which the early Church councils will answer in the affirmative is already formulated by Solomon in the prayer for the dedication of the temple: "Will God indeed dwell with men upon earth?" (1 Kings 8.27). In the context the implication is, of course, that Yahweh does not dwell in the temple in the literal way a primitive mentality imagined, implying also that the god needed to be fed and constantly attended to. But the Hebrew idea of the dwelling of God among men went beyond that of their neighbours. The self-revelation of Yahweh in the Sinaitic covenant was a theophany, but not just an ordinary theophany such as we read of the Canaanite gods to their devotees or even, for example, that granted to Jacob in the shrine at Bethel. It implied a guarantee of the divine presence to the people. It was this promise: "I am with you", "I will be your God", that enabled them to resist the gravitational pull of the pagan religion of the Baalim in Canaan. To enter the covenant was to accept and respond to this presence as a permanent factor in the life of the people.

This presence is expressed in the Old Testament in different ways. The visible locus of the presence in the earliest period is any place where a numinous experience had taken place, such as that of Abraham at Shechem (Gen. 12.7) and of Jacob at Bethel (Gen. 28.11 ff.). Later Israelite thinking identified these manifestations of the numinous with Yahweh, but it is clear that in themselves they were ambiguous and sometimes anonymous. With exodus and covenant, Sinai becomes the definitive locus of Yahweh's self-manifestation. But since the people could not stay for ever around the mountain, how was this presence to be continually experienced? This was especially important in view of the strong pull of the fertility cult in Canaan where the Baalim were already in possession. Elijah found one solution in making a pilgrimage to Sinai where the covenant-theophany was repeated, if in a different way; but for the community as a whole the ark and the tent served as a focus of that divine presence among them which was promised in the covenant. It is often assumed that ark and tent were quite distinct in the early period and that the former was a Canaanite cult-object taken over by Israel. Von Rad has added to this the unproved assumption of a distinct "theology" attached to each. All this is very risky in view of the paucity and uncertainty of our sources on the early cult of Israel, and it is equally possible that from the beginning the ark was in the tent, that is, the tent served as a shelter for the ark, though they were later thought of as separate. The ark in particular symbolized the abiding covenant-presence of Yahweh; after many vicissitudes it was finally brought up to Jerusalem by David (2 Sam. 6) and transferred to the inner sanctuary of the Solomonic temple in a liturgical ceremony in the course of which the question from which we began this survey was asked.

This idea of an abiding presence is seized on and enriched with new insights, drawing upon, elaborating and giving new depth to the basic credal data. Thus the Deuteronomists speak of the covenant as the way Yahweh has chosen to *approach* his people and by which they approach him. They also stress the idea of mediation (Dt. 6.26–31), thus preparing for the mediator of the new covenant, the prophet promised by Moses (Dt. 18.18). The Deuteronomic insistence on one central sanctuary (Dt. 12.5) is also intimately connected with this idea of an abiding presence and is a genuinely ancient ideal, if not always put into practice.

What it declares is that there is but one theophany, one manifestation of the Name, the divine personality which creates community and by which the community lives. From this radiates all that we find in the psalms and the eschatological passages in the prophetic books about Zion as the epicentre of Israel and the world of the nations.

This "God-with-us" theology, however, carried with it its own danger of false security, of using the presence as a cover for irreligious conduct, and it was perhaps against this undesirable by-product of the reform which took place in his youth that Jeremiah is warning in the scene where he pickets the temple and inveighs against the worshippers as they enter (chapter 7). There was also the difficulty felt in the post-exilic period of reconciling this here-and-now presence with the divine transcendence so much stressed in the post-exilic Priestly document. A solution is arrived at in this last strand of the composition of the Old Testament by seeing this covenant-presence as a sacrament of encounter, the focal point between God and man, heaven and earth. The insistence that the tent (= temple) be made according to heavenly specifications and the intensification of the idea of mediation, especially in the Day of Expiation, provided positive elements which were worked into the earliest Christian thinking about the identity of Jesus and thereby dynamically re-interpreted in the New Testament.

In order to see this most primitive incarnational theology in its proper context, which is liturgical, we have to bear in mind first of all what had happened to Jewish liturgy at the time of Christ. We find a clue at once in the first chapters of the gospels where the ministry of the Baptist as messenger and forerunner is presented within the late-Jewish tradition about Elijah deriving, as it seems, from the anonymous prophetic book of Malachi (the title is taken from 3.1, "I will send my messenger", in Hebrew *malaki*). In this book the preparation for the coming of the Messiah is seen as a purification of worship and the ministers of worship culminating in the solemn entry of the Messiah into the temple: "The Lord whom you seek will suddenly come to his temple" (3.1). The threatening language which the Baptist reserves for the Sadducees follows closely the prophet Malachi (Mt. 3.7–12; cf. Mal. 3.3). Only after this cleansing can the self-offering of the nation within the covenant-partnership be acceptable. Irregularities must be set aside so that "all nations will call you blessed, for you will be a land of delight" (Mal. 3.12). The allusions to this theme in the first two chapters of Luke are obvious and inescapable.

We hardly need to trace in detail the process by which the temple liturgy had reached this low point at the time of Christ. A long history of graft and internecine strife, the misdeeds of Onias III and Jason the stooge of Antiochus the Seleucid persecutor, the disappointments following the assumption of the high-priestly office by Simon in 141 B.C., the secularization which went on during the Roman period, led to the conviction shared by many sectors of Judaism that the old order was no longer viable. This is reflected in the literature of the inter-testamentary period: the Book of Jubilees, a work of Pharisee inspiration, the Pharisaic Psalms of Solomon which speak of the need to purify a venal priesthood, the Testament of the Twelve Patriarchs, also basically pharisaic or hasidic, which looks forward to a priestly messiah, all witness to this. According to the latter the priest-messiah will be without sin while the king-messiah "will establish a new priesthood for all the Gentiles" (Test. Levi 8.14). The messiah of Aaron awaited by the Qumran community is also evidently in opposition to the levitical priesthood of the temple with which they would have nothing to do.

This is the background against which we are to understand what some important texts of the New Testament say about the need for a new approach (*prosagōgē*) to God supplanting that of temple-worship, an approach which is to be through Jesus the new temple or, in his own words, "something greater than the temple" (Mt. 12.6).

We can begin our brief survey by looking at the first two chapters of Luke's gospel which begins and ends in the temple. The appearance of the angel to Mary in the privacy of her own house is contrasted with the splendid temple décor of the annunciation to Zachary, the background to which has to be filled in by reference to Daniel and Malachi. Gabriel tells her that "the power of the Most High will overshadow you", using a verb which is a technical theological word in the Old Testament for the overshadowing of the tent by the cloud. It was the same cloud which filled the sanctuary during the dedicatory service of Solomon, and since the cloud is symbolized in the incense used in the temple, once again we have a deliberate contrast with the annunciation to Zachary. This is the language of the *shekinah*, the visible sign of the presence of the invisible God, and it implies that the old order – ark, tent, temple – now gives way to a new dispensation in which Mary symbolizes and is the depositary of the divine presence:

> *et antiquum documentum*
> *novo cedat ritui.*

The worship of the one, eternal God remains; but the medium of this worship has changed, or better, is now finally revealed for what it is. In the closing scene of these chapters, the presentation in the temple, Luke makes the same point in his own allusive way since he tells us, in effect, that the Glory, the *shekinah*, which in Ezekiel leaves the temple before its destruction, now returns at last to its native place – "did you not know that I must be in my Father's house?"

The same rejection of the old liturgical order is found in a much more intransigent form in Stephen's speech in Acts 7. His radical reinterpretation of sacred history implies that the building of the temple was the climax of apostasy, and it was this blasphemy against the temple which resulted in his death, as it had the death of Jesus some few years before. If, as many think, this homily represents a sort of Hellenistic theology in the early Church, we may find signs of it elsewhere, for example in Paul's polemic against "temples made with hands" (Acts 17.24–25). The Samaritans also took a strong line against the liturgy of the temple of Jerusalem, and it is well known how the third and fourth gospels have a special interest in the Samaritan question. There is evidently something of the same current of thought in *Hebrews*, though presented far more systematically and doctrinally. The end of the liturgical, sacrificial order is to perfect the worshipper, to give him access in the fullness of his manhood to God. But the old order with its endless round of cultic acts and of sacrificial butchery was in reality powerless to create such a possibility. This possibility is created for the first time in Jesus the one priest and in the one all-sufficient act which he performed in his dying. The object of Christian existence is "to serve the living God" (9.14), to find access to God through the self-offering of Jesus made "once for all at the end of the age" (9.26).

The world of the Fourth Gospel is very close in many respects to this liturgical current of thinking in the early Church. It is arguable that the whole gospel has, as one of its main aims, to show that Christ fulfils the expectations and hopes implicit in the great Jewish festivals. It is here we come to the heart of the question we are discussing since it is in the Fourth Gospel that we find *the* incarnational formula, and it is couched in liturgical terms:

> The Word became flesh
> and placed his *tent* among us,
> and we have seen his *glory* . . . (1. 14).

This is the same kind of language which we have found in Luke and in fact the prologue of the Fourth Gospel reflects the same milieu as that of Luke: the contrast with the Baptist and between the old order and the new, the *torah* and Christ. The Sign of the Temple (2.14–22) tells us that the risen body of the Lord, mysteriously identified with the new community, is to take the place of the temple as the depositary of the real presence among men. Something of this is found also in the words to the Samaritan woman, "the hour is coming when neither on this mountain nor in Jerusalem will you worship the Father . . . the hour is coming – *and now is* – when the true worshippers will worship the Father in spirit and in truth" (4.21, 23). We have to look elsewhere than to a sacred place for the central meaning and intelligibility of our life in community.

At this point we should sum up briefly what we have seen and draw an at least provisional conclusion. We have seen that liturgy cannot be a marginal or specialist occupation. It is a function of life as a whole, and therefore also Christian life. The Old Testament evolved different models of the sacramental idea of a vital and fertile meeting between men in community. The central idea was the covenant presented according to different theological insights, none of them definitive. Already in Jeremiah (31.31 ff.) it is supposed that the disastrous reality of sin had thwarted this drive to genuine community with the result that a new order of mediation was necessary. The first Christians, living under the lengthening shadow which was to close over the temple, symbol and centre of the old order, saw the fulfilment of this demand in Jesus as the new temple, the *shekinah*, the ineffable divine reality which gives meaning and unity to the life of both individual and community. Here is the point of dynamic unity between human nature which seeks fulfilment through liturgical participation and the divine movement in its direction – the only point: "No one comes to the Father except through me".

This new possibility in Christ creates community because it is effected at the centre of human nature which means that there can be no more barriers. From one point of view the history of the early Church is the history of the assimilation of this truth especially from the racial point of view – Jew and Gentile. But the assimilation is not yet complete by a long way. There is an incident in the life of Paul, touching in a way, which brings this out very well. In the autumn of 58, he was back in Jerusalem after an absence of nine years and lodging in the house of a Cypriot fellow-Christian. One day when in the temple court after performing the rite of purification following on a vow, he was set on by a mob and only the last-minute intervention by Roman troops saved him from a lynching. It was claimed that he had been seen bringing a certain Trophimus, an Ephesian, into the temple, beyond the four-and-a-half-foot wall which divided the court of the Gentiles from the inner court and to pass which for the uncircumcised meant death. Writing to the fellow-citizens of Trophimus three or four years later he still has this incident in mind:

But now you are in Christ Jesus; now, through the blood of Christ, you have been brought close, you who were once so far away. He is our bond of peace; he has made the two nations one, breaking down the wall that was a barrier between us (Eph. 2.13–14, Knox).

The wall was indeed broken down together with the rest of the temple in the war soon to follow. By that time the new approach had already been firmly established.

XIV

The Lamb of God

THE BIBLICAL FIGURE of the lamb is a good example of the decay and death of images. That Jesus is the lamb of God is a biblical affirmation, being used twice by the Baptist and recorded in the Fourth Gospel. Here it must have had a quite definite and precise meaning even if we do not succeed in discovering what that meaning was. But to compare Jesus in a straightforward way with this gentle, inoffensive and rather foolish animal is quite another thing and results in an unseemly parody far removed from the figure who lives on the pages of the gospel. It has also contributed not a little to some degenerate iconography both of the child Jesus and the man – the usual oleograph of the Sacred Heart, for example. This is worlds apart from what we find in the earliest examples of Christian art, for example in the Catacombs of Callixtus from the third century. Truer to the gospel portrait would be the "man of men" of Ezra Pound's "Ballad of the Goodly Fere" which invites us to recall the authority which subdued both the storm and the fury of the possessed man whom no one else could approach, the authority before which the vendors in the temple precincts cowered. And then the manner of his death:

> The hounds of the silver sky gave tongue
> But never a cry cried he!

It is in fact paradoxical that the Isaian comparison with the lamb "led to the slaughter", whether we consider it apt or no, points to the heroic and silent acceptance of suffering and death.

It is already something to have got this distracting and corrupting image out of the mind, but can we recover the original sense of the description of Jesus as the lamb of God? Let us see what the texts themselves say.

The Baptist, as we have seen, twice points to Jesus as the lamb of God, on the first occasion adding: "who takes away the sin of the world" (Jn. 1.29, 36). This occurs in a discourse dealing with baptism though there is no account of the baptism of Jesus, perhaps on account of this being presumed as known from the Synoptics or local tradition. The same process of going on to bring out deeper levels of meanings can be detected in passages referring to the Agony in the Garden and the Last Supper. The Baptist attests that he saw the Spirit descend like a dove and remain on him (1.32). What, then, did he mean by the lamb of God? There is nothing in the Synoptic baptism-account about a lamb, and yet presumably he intended his words to be understood, if indeed he said them. At first reading, reference to either the paschal lamb or the Isaian lamb seems improbable since it raises the question as to how the Baptist could have recognized right at the beginning of the ministry that Jesus was destined for a violent death, and one moreover which was to have an expiatory and redemptive character. And if his words were so understood, why the shock and scandal at the great turning-point of the ministry, after the confession of Peter, when Jesus solemnly announced his forthcoming death?

As always, we have to begin looking for a solution within the context of the gospel as a whole. No one supposes that we have in the Fourth Gospel a verbatim report of the words spoken by the characters who appear on its pages, not even of Jesus himself. They all speak the same exalted, theological, Johannine language, the kind that we find also in the three epistles. It is even impossible at times to tell where the *oratio recta* ends and the comment of the evangelist begins, as with the discourse to Nicodemus. This might lead us to take a second look at the words of the Baptist.

We know that this gospel represents the death of Jesus as the fulfilment of the Jewish passover. It is arguable in fact that the gospel sets out to show that the aspirations implicit in the great Jewish festivals are fulfilled in Jesus the Messiah. After speaking of the death on the cross, the evangelist goes on to tell us that his legs were not broken, a minor circumstance in itself, but recorded in all probability as the fulfilment of a prescription as regards the lamb of the passover supper (Jn. 19.36, cf. Ex. 12.46). In the passion story as a whole, our attention is directed to the fact that, as the official Jewish passover was getting under way and the priests were observing the pre-passover rules for ritual purity, the true passover was being celebrated outside on the cross. That this way of thinking of the death of Jesus was familiar before this time can be seen in Paul's reference to Jesus as "our passover lamb" (1 Cor. 5.7).

Within this context of the understanding of Christ and his mission in the Fourth Gospel the saying of the Baptist is therefore fully intelligible. We should also note that it is a basic theme of the Johannine writings that Christ came to take away sin. So, in explanation of his affirmation that "you will know the truth and the truth will set you free" he adds:

> Truly, I say to you, every one who commits sin is a slave to sin. The slave does not continue in the house for ever; the son continues for ever. So if the Son makes you free (from sin), you will be free indeed (8. 34–36).

And in the First Epistle:

> You know that he appeared to take away sins, and in him there is no sin (3. 5).
> The reason the Son of God appeared was to destroy the works of the devil (3. 8).

In the light of this, the saying of the Baptist could be read as a summary of the mission of Jesus, put right at the beginning of the gospel in the mouth of the herald, pointing straight to the centre, the heart of the Christian message as understood by the evangelist. We *know* that the Baptist in some way indicated the mission of Jesus. We do not know in what terms he did so, nor perhaps did John the Evangelist. Here as elsewhere we have to leave room for the interpretative function of the writer.

There is, however, another source from which the image of the lamb entered early Christian tradition which may help us to define more exactly the original meaning of the designation as used by the Baptist. The last of the four Isaian Servant Songs speaks of a mysterious passion-figure who suffers hatred, physical

violence, disfigurement and death, all of which he accepts freely
and in silence. Of him we read that

> He was oppressed, and he was afflicted,
> yet he opened not his mouth;
> like a lamb that is led to the slaughter,
> like a sheep that before its shearers is dumb,
> so he opened not his mouth (Is. 53. 7).

It was inevitable that the suffering Christ should have been seen
as fulfilling this prophetic figure. Philip evangelized the Sudanese
official "beginning from this scripture text" (Acts 8.35), it is
behind the reference in the First Epistle of Peter to the ransom
brought about "with the precious blood of Christ, like that of a
lamb without blemish or spot" (1.19), and John himself quotes
from the fourth Servant Song in his gospel (12.38). It could hardly
have been absent from the mind of Christ when he spoke, at the
Last Supper, of "the blood of the covenant which is poured out
for many" since the Servant also "poured out his soul to death"
and "bore the sins of many". Does this throw any light on the
Baptist's exclamation?

We saw earlier that the whole discourse in the first chapter of
John's gospel corresponds to the baptism-scene in the earlier
gospels, and behind both there lies the idea of a servant called to
a mission. The voice from heaven, "Behold my son, the Beloved,
in whom I am well pleased" echoes the opening words of the
first Isaian Servant Song:

> Behold my servant whom I uphold,
> my chosen one in whom I delight (42.1).

The descent of the Spirit, which the Baptist also claims to have
witnessed, is that spoken of in the next line of the same poem:

> I have put my Spirit upon him,
> he will bring forth justice to the nations.

It is, at least in the understanding of early Christian tradition, the
same servant who, in the fourth song, is led like a lamb to the
slaughter. The line of thought between Baptist and Evangelist

is therefore firmly established. We can therefore conclude that it would be natural for the evangelist to complete the line of thought by dramatically anticipating the revelation of the vicarious suffering and death of Jesus right from the first page of the gospel, and we can do this without having recourse to the frequently assumed but never proved hypothesis of a play on an Aramaic word meaning both "lamb" and "servant".

We might add that the lamb which features so regularly in Christian art, especially in some of its more debased forms, sometimes carrying a banner or looking down with a rather jaundiced expression from a turret or wall, is the animal mentioned so often in the Book of Revelation. It derives from the to us incredibly confused zoology of Jewish apocalytic writing. A lamb that never was: slain and yet alive, with seven horns and seven eyes, that opens a book and in whose blood clothes can be washed white, which is capable of wrath, which can become a shepherd – all of this and more besides makes the writings of the apocalyptics a difficult world indeed to enter. We know from the Enoch literature and the Testaments of the Twelve Patriarchs that the lamb was a symbol of the victorious Messiah. Here in the canonical Apocalypse we have a combination of the sacrificial passover lamb and the apocalyptic symbol, the messianic king "who was slain and who lives for ever". In a time of extreme crisis, perhaps the persecution of Domitian, it expressed for Christians who were familiar with this kind of writing the conviction that the risen Lord was present in his suffering Church and that no evil could touch them.

The way back to the biblical understanding of Christ is not always easy. Apart from the difficulty involved in listening to men belonging to a different culture, age and language-group, we prefer the comfortable security of our own diluted and adapted religious ideas. But if we are Christian at all, if we believe that what we are listening to is a word of God addressed to us, no effort should be beyond the compass of our will.

XV

The Church's Mission in Saint Luke's Gospel

EVEN IF we had no other source of information, we could easily guess, from a reading of the Third Gospel alone, that it was written by a missionary. This emerges more clearly if we bear in mind, as we have to, that it is the first part of a two-volume work which was meant to be read in its entirety. The references to Luke in early Christian literature, including the correspondence of Paul, examined in the light of the excerpts from a travelogue in the first person in Acts, suggest the conclusion that this gospel comes from Antioch, *the* missionary centre of the early days. We are told almost casually that it was at Antioch that certain Cyrenaean and Cypriot Christians first achieved the breakthrough, so momentous in its consequences, of addressing the message directly to non-Jews, and Luke writes here like a man who had been personally involved in the events he narrates. If we go further, as several scholars of repute are prepared to do, and identify the Luke of tradition with the Cyrenaean prophet-catechist Lucius of the Antioch church mentioned in Acts 13.1, we are led to the interesting conclusion that Luke–Acts, the most considerable literary composition of the New Testament by any reckoning, was written by an African who settled in Asia and was one of the first missionaries to Europe.

The distinctive feature of the Third Gospel compared with the others is the long travel-narrative which takes up the central section of the gospel. Its importance can be gauged by the solemn tone of the introductory words:

As the time approached when he was to be taken up to heaven, he set his face resolutely towards Jerusalem and sent messengers ahead (9. 51).

A journey away from one's homeland is one of the most persistent motifs in the Scriptures, and indeed in world literature. Witness the journey of Gilgamesh towards the discovery of death, the journey in search of the Grail, Abraham and the people of Israel towards the land, Jesus to Jerusalem. Luke, a good part of whose life had been spent as a missionary on the move, gives great importance to this journey. He sees it as a figure of the Church with a mission which had to be accomplished, a definite goal which had to be reached. At the same time, it provides him with a good framework for the instruction of prospective missionaries and catechists. There is no need to choose between Luke the historian composing "an account of the events which have happened among us" and Luke the catechist and missionary writing for a definite Christian community after the first missions had been accomplished. Bearing in mind the history of the Antioch missionary expeditions, starting with that of Barnabas and Paul, it is not difficult to imagine the impact of such sayings as the following on those training for the mission in Antioch:

> Foxes have their holes, the birds their roosts; but the Son of Man has nowhere to lay his head (9.58).

> Leave the dead to bury their dead; you must go and announce the Kingdom of God (9.60).

> No one who sets his hand to the plough and then keeps on looking back is fit for the Kingdom of God (9.62).

Is not that just what John Mark, an acquaintance of Luke's, had run the risk of doing?

There are also in this section of the gospel specific instructions for the seventy (seventy-two in some manuscripts) whom the Lord sent out in pairs (9.1). The relevance of these for early Christian missionaries becomes clear if we bear in mind that, according to a Jewish reckoning of that time based on the list in Genesis 10, the number of the nations of the world was seventy (seventy-two in the Greek Bible). Moreover, early Christian missionaries operated as a rule in twos – Barnabas and Paul, Paul and Silas, Barnabas and John Mark, as also did the disciples of

John the Baptist. They are instructed to travel light, avoid dilly-dallying on the way, go to their destination and set up one central base of operations. They must above all speak the Word without fear. Risk is an inherent part of the life of a Christian missionary. Those who had been through the mill and, back at Antioch, stood listening to the lector in the weekly assembly, would be hearing of their own experiences:

> When you are brought before synagogues and state authorities, do not begin worrying about how you will conduct your defence or what you will say. For when the time comes the Holy Spirit will instruct you what to say (12.11–12).

> You will be brought before synagogues and put in prison; you will be haled before kings and governors for your allegiance to me. This will be your opportunity to testify. So make up your minds not to prepare your defence beforehand, because I myself will give you power of utterance and a wisdom which no opponent will be able to resist or refute . . . some of you will be put to death (21.12–16).

Was this not literally true of Stephen whose prayer of forgiveness at the point of death repeats that of the Lucan Christ? The element of risk runs through the whole of this gospel, especially in the travel-narrative, but with the risk there comes also the word of assurance:

> To you who are my friends I say: Do not fear those who kill the body and after that they have nothing more they can do (12.4).

In this regard it might be considered strange that Luke, who is generally considered, in the expression of Dante, "the scribe of the meekness of Christ", should take this element of risk inherent in total commitment to its extreme point. He does so because he sees the Church not so much as a fixed and settled society, an institution, but as a mission. Church membership, therefore, involves breaking with the settled routine of a purely natural existence and being called out on a dangerous adventure. Once you begin, there is no question of turning back:

> If anyone comes to me and does not hate his father and mother,

wife and children, brothers and sisters, even his own life, he cannot
be a disciple of mine.

No one who does not carry his cross and come with me can be a
disciple of mine.

None of you can be a disciple of mine without taking leave of all his
possessions (14.26, 27, 33).

It follows that taking part in the Church's mission is not confined
to a minority but is an indispensable condition of Christian
discipleship.

It is clear from this, at any rate, that both volumes of Luke's
work reflect his missionary experience while at the same time
serving as a manual for prospective catechists and missionaries
of a Christian community such as that at Antioch. This could be
pursued further if space permitted. We could, for example, read
the account of the miraculous haul of fish, the occasion of Peter's
missionary call (Lk. 5.1–11) in the light of the "Acts of Peter"
in the second volume. The conversion of Cornelius is in fact the
first "catch" in the deeper waters of the Gentile world into which
the mission had only recently been launched. It is not, however,
just a case of individual Christian missionaries. Luke sees the
Church as in its essence a mission to the world. The Church is the
new Israel, "the Israel of God" as the most distinguished of
Luke's colleagues put it. But in Luke's day, at least before the
destruction of the Jewish state, the current image was that of a
secular kingdom sitting in judgment on and condemning the
world of the pagan nations. Was the Christian Church to be this
kind of Israel? "Lord", ask the disciples after the resurrection,
"is this the time when you are to establish once again the
sovereignty of Israel?" (Acts 1.6). The answer is neither Yes
nor No – "it is not for you to know", it is not for you to speak of
power and rule. You have to go on a journey to the ends of the
earth and keep going until the journey and the task is complete.
Then, and not till then, it will be time to talk about the kingdom.

Luke goes behind the current image of Israel the Church to one
which was older and at that time to a large extent forgotten, that
of Israel exiled and humiliated among the nations, the Israel of

the Servant Songs of Isaiah. Jesus represented his mission as that of the suffering Servant of God, and as Luke makes clear, his journey to Jerusalem is itself a mission, a movement which leads to humiliation, defeat and death:

> I must be on my way today and tomorrow and the next day, because it is unthinkable for a prophet to meet his death anywhere but in Jerusalem (13.33).

The mission of the Church in the world follows the same pattern. There is nothing remotely triumphalist about Luke's idea of the Church. It is the Church exiled, the Church of the dispersion, an image compounded of the many table-fellowships in which he himself had shared off the back streets of the great cities of the Empire. It would hardly be an exaggeration to say that there are some aspects of this image which can be seen more clearly today than at any time since the days of Luke. Thus, if the Church is in fact what Luke implies that it is, we cannot compare it with a secular, political power-structure. It will in fact be the opposite of this:

> In the world kings lord it over their subjects; and those in authority are called their country's "Benefactors". Not so with you. On the contrary, the highest among you must bear himself like the youngest, the chief of you like a servant (22.24–26).
>
> The least among you – he is the greatest (9.48).

It will also be the poor Church and the Church of the poor. The fact that Luke stresses this more than the other evangelists is precisely because of his starting-point in the mission to mankind. The missionary must go barefoot and carry no purse (10.3) precisely because he is going into a world where social injustice thrives and where, in Luke's day as now, the majority live in a dehumanizing poverty. This explains why he alone records the startling injunction of the Baptist:

> The man with two shirts must share with him who has none, and anyone who has food must do the same (3.10).

Where Matthew has "blessed are the poor in spirit" Luke has simply "the poor" and adds a corresponding woe on the rich to make the point more clearly. He alone has found room for the telling stories of the Rich Man and Lazarus and the Rich Fool, the latter ending with the moral:

> That is how it is with the man who amasses wealth for himself and remains a pauper in the eyes of God (12.21)

The inability of the rich young man to part with his great possessions led to the reflection: "How hard it is for the wealthy to enter the kingdom of God!" – as thought-provoking a reflection for us today as it must have been for Theophilus since he too presumably was "a man of the ruling class".

Luke's gospel is full of these straws in the wind, pointers to the true nature of the missionary Church never so relevant as at the present day. He does not see it as an *imperium in imperio*, a solid mass like a foreign body in the world. The Church must be not over against the world but in it like the seed in the ground and the yeast in the dough (13.18–21). The goal is a new unity of the kind outlined by Luke's missionary companion Paul:

> There is no such thing as Jew and Greek, slave and freeman, male and female; for you are all one person in Christ Jesus (Gal. 3.28).

The Church's mission as envisaged by Luke is to remove barriers. There is no distinction by reason of wealth and social class. This he makes quite clear. There is none certainly which is racial – and we should remember in this regard that the question of Jewish relations with the Samaritans in which he was so interested was essentially racial. Church membership for Luke was meant to give a new vitality and a new impulse to personal relationships. Alas, how seldom that really happens! Above all, it should give a sense of purpose, since the Christian is a man with a mission, a goal towards which to contribute in society, completing the world and sharing in the involvement and suffering of God in the world which is inseparable from this.

XVI

A New Kind of Priesthood

THE REFORMERS of the sixteenth century are not the only ones who noticed that the New Testament has very little about priesthood and priests and that the term *priest* is never used there of any individual Christian. There is consequently nothing about a clergy–lay division and the few eucharistic assemblies which are described look rather different from ours with their clear delimitation of the respective roles of priest and layman. To whom, moreover, is the command to *do this,* that is, to observe the memorial-service of the Lord's death, addressed – to the Twelve and subsequent Church-leaders only or inclusively to the whole new Israel of God of whom the Twelve are representatives by the very fact of being twelve?

If we turn to the letters of St Paul we find little if anything of the priestly, in the vaguely pejorative sense in which the adjective is generally employed. After reading the account of the shipwreck-eucharist off Malta (if it was a eucharist) and that other in the second-storey room at Troas, we might wonder how he would have coped with a solemn High Mass with incense, prostrations, kissings and the rest, or indeed what he would have thought of it.

In the context of the Jewish world of that time, Christianity emerged as from the start a lay-movement and Jesus as a layman who was set on by the priesthood and whose execution was on the score of an attack on the Holy in the form of a blasphemy against the temple than which nothing holier could be conceived. At the same time, we know that he purposed to fulfil, not destroy, the old order (that is, the Law) and the priesthood was an important part of that old order. This makes it urgent to discover what happens to the Jewish idea of priesthood in Christianity. The caste system disappears finally with the destruction of the temple, yet the priestly idea or ideal is fulfilled on a deeper level than that of institution, just as the *torah* is fulfilled but only at the price of a radical transformation (see Mt. 5.17 ff.). It will evidently be of interest to us to know in what way.

It so happens that only in one writing of the New Testament is Jesus spoken of as priest, and that not one of the better known, the Epistle to the Hebrews. It is used surprisingly little in the liturgy despite the riches of teaching which it contains; only seventeen of its three hundred-odd verses occur in the liturgical cycle, divided between a short passage in the third Mass for Christmas Day (usually recited privately) and another on the first Sunday in Passiontide. One suspects, moreover, that the priesthood of Christ is not often made the subject of a homily. The unknown author wrote to strengthen the faith of a particular group of Christians who were in all probability fairly recent converts from Judaism. From the large part which the priesthood plays in it some have supposed that it was addressed to convert Jewish priests – possibly the "many priests" who accepted baptism according to Acts 6.7. Scholars were not slow to notice some striking similarities between this epistle and the writings of the Qumran community. This latter, almost certainly Essene, was at any rate well and truly priest-ridden and lacking in the charismatic character of the early Christian community. *A propos* of the subject under discussion, we should note that they awaited the coming of three distinct eschatological figures: the messiah of David (a king), the messiah of Aaron (a priest) and the prophet promised by Moses (in Dt. 18.18). In their Holy Rule they are told that they must

> depart from none of the counsels of the Law to walk in the stubbornness of their hearts, but must be ruled by the primitive precepts in which the men of the community were first instructed until there shall come the Prophet and the Messiahs of Aaron and Israel.

These three figures are brought together and merged in Christ in the New Testament and particularly in Hebrews. In keeping with this, the prophetic and priestly roles are simultaneously present in the community founded by Christ – not one part prophetic (the laity) and the other priestly (the priesthood) but *all* prophetic and *all* priestly. This is the starting-point for the specifically Christian understanding of what priesthood means and what it is for.

How then does the New Testament change the idea of priest and priesthood current in Judaism at that time? As with the sayings of Jesus on Old Testament law, there is a process of radicalization. We have to begin by asking what priesthood is for. Approach to God in the Old Testament and in Judaism was through ritual acts, especially sacrificial ritual, generally carried out by priests. They were mediators, and it was through them that the people entered into the Presence. This was particularly true of the great Day of Expiation and the ceremonial act which took place on it. Since the author of Hebrews makes much of this we had better look at it a little more closely.

To understand, in the first place, what *yom kippur* meant to those who took part in it (and indeed continue to do so, though the manner has changed) we have to bear in mind that tremendous and, for us, almost obsessive consciousness of sin and guilt which Old Testament man harboured and which found moving expression in psalms of repentance like the too-well known "Out of the Depths" (the dark and dangerous depths of the psyche, if we can forget the "Holy Souls" for a moment). Sin down there, in the depths, made it impossible to come into God's presence, *to see the Face*. Hence a whole round of cultic acts designed to exorcize the feeling of guilt, to cleanse the depths of the soul. The culmination of all these was the Day of Expiation when the high priest and he alone entered the inner sanctuary and on this one day of the year, taking with him the blood of the sacrificed animal for the sacramental removal of sin. This is the point at which Hebrews radicalizes the Old Testament idea of priesthood. *Yom kippur* is used as a kind of allegory of the one all-sufficient priestly act of Christ. The temple is heaven, the entering into the inner sanctuary by the high priest as the representative of the community is the ascension of Jesus into heaven, the sacrificial blood is the blood of the Cross:

> When Christ appeared as a high priest of the good things that have come, then through the greater and more perfect tent . . . he entered

once for all into the Holy Place, taking not the blood of goats and calves but his own blood, thus securing an eternal redemption (9.11–12).

It would appear that the ripping aside of the temple curtain recorded by the evangelists at the death of Christ is part of this same theological presentation of the meaning of the death which had just occurred. From this moment all can draw near:

> Since we have confidence to enter the sanctuary by the blood of Jesus, by the new and living way which he opened for us through the curtain, that is, through his flesh, and since we have a great priest over the house of God, let us draw near with a true heart in full assurance of faith (10.19–22).

What is implied is that there is no longer any place for a priestly caste but one priest and mediator only who has done *once for all,* in one single act, what the multiplicity of cultic acts of the old order could not achieve:

> – nor was it to offer himself repeatedly, as the high priest enters the Holy Place yearly with blood not his own; for then he would have had to suffer repeatedly since the foundation of the world. But as it is, he has appeared *once for all* at the end of the age to put away sin by the sacrifice of himself (9.25–26).

This once-for-all character of the act is often stressed in this epistle. Whether we in the Roman Catholic tradition, with our tendency to emphasize the quantitative aspect (two Masses better than one, etc.) and our practice of stipended Masses have fully come to terms with it is another question.

With this radicalization there went necessarily a reinterpretation of the Holy. As long as a well-defined sphere of the Holy is conceived of, concentrated in a certain place, the tent and then the temple, you need a priestly caste to take charge of it and see that it doesn't get mixed up with the profane, everyday realities of life. The Jewish conviction that there was such a sphere explains their superstitious attachment to the temple; and readers of Jeremiah chapter 7 will see that Jesus was not the first to attack this idea. It also explains the excessive preoccupation with ritual and rubrics: the smearing of blood on the tip of the right ear and the big toe of the right foot, eating the correct portions of the slaughtered animals' entrails, and the like. Worse still, it encouraged a strong penal note and heavy punishments for purely ritual faults. In the Priestly Document there are quite a few people who, literally, drop dead.

Perhaps most important of all, however, the existence of a priestly caste dictates the idea of a layman. You can have laymen only if you have priests first, and as a historical fact we do not hear of laymen (*laici*) in the Church until after a separate clerical order (*clerici*) had emerged. It is particularly significant for our theme that only in the Priestly Document do we find a word for *layman* in the Old Testament. He is defined negatively, from the point of view of the priest, as a non-priest, one who does not belong to a priestly family. Both in the Hebrew (the word is *ʒar*) and in the Greek (*allogenes*) the meaning is, literally, *stranger* (R.S.V. sometimes translates appropriately *outsider*!). There was no way of crossing the boundary from one class to the other. In fact we find in Numbers 3.10 the death penalty threatened on any layman "trying his vocation". They solved the problem of vocations by not having any.

In the new and final order all this is radically changed. The saying about the temple in John 2.19–21, as explained by the evangelist, implies that the centre is no longer a building, a definite locus, but his body, the Body of Christ which is the new community. This community is both prophetic and priestly throughout, as we have seen. It is "built on the foundation of the apostles and prophets" and it is "a kingdom of priests, a holy nation". This of course does not imply that each individual Christian has to think of himself as a priest. Whoever he is or whatever his station, he shares in Christ's priesthood only in so far as he belongs to the community. It is the *belonging* that counts.

Only when we have grasped this should we go on to speak of the ministerial priesthood. Failure to observe this due priority leads to the same kind of distortion as thinking of papal infallibility without reference to its function in the life of the whole Spirit-filled community. This works out in different ways. As implied at the beginning, it is misleading to interpret the command given at the Last Supper as addressed exclusively to the Twelve and, after them, ordained ministers, and not also to the whole community which carries out the remembrance by eating and drinking. It is equally misleading to speak of the Spirit sent on the disciples for the forgiveness of sins without reference to the pentecostal outpourings of the Spirit on the whole community. Likewise to speak of "binding and loosing" with regard to Peter, neglecting the same authorization made to the whole community of disciples, the Church in embryo (Mt. 18.18). According to Roman Catholic teaching the Sacrament of Order restricts the consecration of the eucharistic bread and wine and the sacramental forgiveness of sins to a certain limited number of the community. This is therefore conceived of as an authorization by Christ. This does not mean that we cannot also see in it some form of delegation by the community, a means by which the community articulates its existence as a visible society. It is, in other words, not just vicarious (the *sacerdos alter Christus* idea) but representational. The authorization in any case is not well described as *a power*, in the sense in which some of the dogmatic textbooks speak of the power over the natural body and the mystical body, language as misleading as it is unscriptural.

If we still have a cleric–lay problem awaiting solution in the post-conciliar age – and we surely have – it is because we have not taken in the message of Hebrews or understood sufficiently the radical transformation of the idea of priesthood which it implies. There are many today who are wondering whether our present system involving a priesthood mostly trained apart, organized apart, even playing golf together apart, is the best calculated to enable the Church to mediate Christ to the world. Here as elsewhere a solution will come only through returning to the sources and taking seriously what we find there.

XVII

Mary, The Church and the Kerygma

SPEAKING OF THE Virgin Mary within the context of the mystery of the Church (chapter eight of the constitution *Lumen Gentium*) may prove to have been the most important of all the steps the Council has taken towards eventual reconciliation between the Churches – provided that it is logically and courageously followed up. What this means for Catholics will be understood if we recall that in the textbooks of theology the tractate on Mariology (may we hope finally to bury this ugly word?) has always followed that on the Word Incarnate and remained without any real relation at all to teaching on the Church (*de Ecclesia*). What it means for other Christians remains to be seen, but our way of speaking of dogmas such as the Assumption will at least be a little more intelligible if not necessarily convincing. One recalls the mixture of exasperation and despair with which the proclamation of the dogma of the Assumption was greeted. It was widely seen either as a typical Roman example of deductive theological rationalization *in vacuo* (the *potuit, decuit ergo fecit* kind) or as a capitulation to popular pressure. In view of the profound change of feeling within the Roman Catholic Church in the last score of years, we can more easily admit that the line of argument taken up by apologists after the event did not look very convincing, principally due to the way the Scripture–Tradition question was presented or presupposed.

To state the problem is simple enough. How can the Assumption of the Virgin be proposed to Christians as of faith divine and revealed, to which assent must be given under pain of eternal reprobation, if it is nowhere mentioned in the Scriptures and is neither a part of nor a necessary deduction from the apostolic kerygma, the faith laid down once for all and delivered to the saints? Whatever line of argument is taken, we are at least driven to relate Mary to the mystery of the Church in its total reality and not to think of her, as we have for so long been used to doing, as just a human person in intimate relation with her son. One corollary of this close relation between Mary and the mystery of the Church is that we must relate what the Scriptures say of her to the central statement of faith, the apostolic kerygma proclaimed to the world at Pentecost and in the years following. Inspiration, however we define it, does not mean that every statement found in the New Testament and in the gospels in particular has an absolute and autonomous value either as fact or judgment. Everything has to be judged not in accordance with absolute canons imposed by ourselves and imported into the Scriptures but in relation to this primary statement of faith, what we can call the kerygmatic centre. This will also apply to what we find written about Mary. We shall therefore try in what follows to state as clearly as possible, and in order, what has come down to us about her in the apostolic writings, resisting the temptation of a facile concordism by reducing everything to a homogeneous unity where in fact there is no unity. We shall also try not to go beyond what we find in the texts.

1. She is not mentioned at all in *New Testament letters* with the exception of the embryonic credal phrase of Paul about Christ "born of the seed of David, born of a woman" (Gal. 4.4). Here, as in later creeds, it is a question only of establishing the human descent of Christ and there is no elaboration about who the woman was.

2. According to the established critical position of today, the first stage of gospel formation is found in Mark and the sections common to Matthew and Luke which are not in Mark and which are presumed to derive from a lost Sayings-book. In this primitive record Mary is mentioned by name as the mother of Jesus, though possibly in a way designed by the speakers to discredit her son, since the Jews always trace descent from the father and the mention of the mother may be interpreted as implying that the

father was unknown (Mk. 6.3; Mt. 13.55). There is also the episode in which some of his relatives, including his mother, tried to get through the crowds to speak to him, provoking the question: "Who is my mother? Who are my brothers?" And looking around at those who were sitting in the circle around him (Matthew says they were disciples), he said: "Here are my mother and my brothers! Whoever does the will of God is my brother, my sister, my mother" (Mk. 3.31–5; Mt. 13.46–50; Lk. 8.19–21).

That is all that we find in the Synoptic record of the ministry. No Synoptic mentions Mary in the list of women who were present on Calvary and there is no record of any apparition of the risen Lord to her. As we shall see in a moment, Luke tells us that she was present with other relatives of the Lord and the apostles before Pentecost, after which no more is heard of her in the canonical writings. The apocrypha, in which stories about her occur, do not inspire confidence as historical records and neither of the rival traditions which locate her last days respectively at Ein Karem near Jerusalem and Ephesus in Turkey can be accepted uncritically. The latter in particular has little to recommend it, despite the visions of Catherine Emmerich and the publicity of the Turkish Tourist Board, and it must seem somewhat strange that Paul, who lived in Ephesus for three years, never speaks in his correspondence written to the church in that city or from it to Corinth of Mary having lived or died there.

3. The Infancy narratives in Matthew and Luke represent the last stage of the formation of the written gospels and they are therefore the furthest removed from the kerygmatic centre. Though they speak of events, they are not events in the same way as the ones referred to above. The attitude of the writer is different and the element of theological or midrashic reflection is uppermost. Above all, the writers of these chapters are not concerned with supplying biographical data on Mary. They think and write of her and her role in the divine plan in theological, that is, scriptural language: as the virgin-daughter of Zion who is to bring forth the messiah in accordance with prophecy, as the ark of the covenant which contains the Shekinah, the Presence, as the tent in which man meets his God. We should note in

particular how in the Annunciation scene Luke shows her as the model of Christian discipleship by the way in which she receives the Word. This reception of the Word in the mind and will is the condition of her reception of the Word in her body. In this he remains faithful to the order of priorities laid down by Jesus himself in the saying referred to above. Her motherhood is dependent on her discipleship, not *vice versa*. She is therefore in a very real sense the first of those who "hear the word of God and keep it".

4. In the Johannine writings Mary is already clearly discerned as "the type and excellent exemplar" of the Church (*Lumen Gentium,* par. 53). The Woman of Cana and Golgotha is given archetypal significance in the symbolic representation of the sacramental reality of the Church, present at the beginning and the end of the ministry. We have therefore in the canonical Scriptures the beginning of what we shall find later in a much expanded form in writers like Justin and Irenaeus: Mary as the new Woman, representative and prototype of a new, redeemed humanity, as Eve was of the old. This was simply a new application of a process found throughout the Scriptures, the idea of corporate personality, implying the interrelation of individual and group: Jacob-Israel, Adam-mankind. The same type of thinking is behind the Sign of the Woman in the Apocalypse (chapter 12). It seems likely that Luke also wished to draw our attention to this ecclesial role of Mary by representing the Spirit coming down upon both her and the gathered community at the beginning of his gospel and of Acts. This intention will be seen the more clearly if we bear in mind that these two make up one work as regards both plan and structure.

We can sum all this up by saying that of all the things which were certainly known about Mary in the apostolic age only one is given prominence in the writings which have survived, namely, the fact that she listened to the Word and accepted it by an absolutely free and personal response. By this acceptance she was able to play a special part in the development of God's "hidden purpose" (Eph. 3.9) in the working out of the one prophetic history, first prefigured in sign in the old dispensation, then present in reality in Christ and the Church. It is on this basis that the Constitution *Lumen Gentium* speaks of Mary and the Church as part of the same mystery of salvation:

> The Church indeed, contemplating her (Mary's) hidden sanctity, imitating her charity and faithfully fulfilling the Father's will, by receiving the Word of God in faith becomes herself a mother; for by her preaching and by baptism she brings forth to a new and immortal life children conceived of the holy Spirit and born of God. She is also a virgin since she preserves integrally and purely the promise made to her spouse. In imitation of the mother of her Lord, she keeps with virginal purity an entire faith, a firm hope and a sincere charity by the power of the Holy Spirit (par. 64).

It is only by keeping firmly before us this mutual inherence that we can avoid the kind of exaggerations to which we have been so prone in the past. So, for example, if the Assumption is to have any truly Christian meaning at all, it must be understood not just of Mary in the presence of God, the first of the saints, but of her being there as the sign and assurance of the final success of God's plan for the world of which the Church is the instrument. Death and corruption cannot have the last word.

And to dispel any facile optimism, let us add that she is also the model for the wayfaring Church since we are told of her that, although she did not understand some things that were said to her, she continued to ponder them in her heart.

K

XVIII

The Ascension as Mystery
of Salvation

IT IS RATHER EASY to think of the Ascension as a relatively
unimportant appendix to the paschal mystery of death and rising,
the curtain on the drama of the *triduum sanctum*. All the more so
that we find embarrassing the account of a physical movement
upwards from a certain spot on this planet towards a goal somewhere "up there", providentially hidden in cloud, and disturbing
the fact that ascensions (or assumptions) occur with some frequency in ancient literature, from Henoch and Elijah to Julius
Caesar and Mohammed.

This impression might be strengthened when we note that the
Ascension features hardly at all in the earlier Christian preaching
of the Good News. It is absent, for example, from the list of those
things traditioned to Paul as of first importance and which he in
his turn passed on as the essence of the Christian message (in
1 Cor. 15.3–8). The early churches, moreover, dispensed with any
liturgical commemoration of this event and in any case the
emphasis soon slipped on to the secondary aspect of physical
locomotion. This may be seen in the basilica erected in the fourth
century on the Mount of Olives, represented in the contemporary
absidal mosaic of Santa Pudenziana, which had a hole in the roof
for Christ to pass through.

According to the earliest and therefore basic view in the New
Testament, the vindication of the dead Jesus, his glorification, his
presence to the Father, takes place at the moment of the Resurrection. In the long last chapter of Luke there is nothing to
suggest that his separation from them did not take place on Easter
day, and this account lies behind that in the textually uncertain

conclusion of Mark. The Christ of the Fourth Gospel commissions Mary of Magdala on Easter morning to tell the disciples that he is ascending to his father there and then. He is with his Father already, in that entirely new dimension of the risen life; he is therefore *already* in heaven.

Only once do we read of the Ascension as an event, in Luke's account in Acts. Here it is important to note that the author's starting-point and his main interest throughout is *the experience and communication of the Spirit*. As we know from the story he tells, he had had experience of this in the churches which he had visited or in which he had lived. This explains why the gift of ecstatic utterance, or the special form which this took in "speaking with tongues", occurs in his account of the first liturgical gathering with which the history of the Christian Church begins (Acts 2.4). In view of Luke's interest in liturgy it is not at all improbable that he has articulated his conviction about the Spirit as the foundation of Church life in a liturgical form and given this paradigmatic value by making it a first event. There is the Scripture reading (from Joel), the homily, the exercise of the charismatic gifts (we know from 1 Cor. 12–14 that they were exercised during divine service) – a complete liturgy of the Word. It was, we recall, at Antioch during divine service that Agabus prophesied, and Luke was present on that occasion (Acts 16.27 in the Western text).

The Ascension of Jesus issues in the giving, the pouring out of the Spirit. In this context it was natural that Luke, being a deeply scriptural Christian as well as a very allusive writer, should recall the taking up of the prophet Elijah. He shows interest in this figure at several points of his two-volume work. He uses of Jesus the same term that the Greek Old Testament uses for the taking up of the prophet (both were "assumed", 2 Kings 2.11; Lk. 9.51; Acts 1.2). The clothing with power from on high recalls Elijah's disciple clothed with his master's mantle with which he works miracles (cf. the miracles which follow at once in Acts). The earnest upward gaze of the disciples on Olivet reminds us of the condition which Elijah imposed on his disciple if he was to receive the Spirit, namely, that he should *see* him as he was being taken up (2 Kings 2.10).

Luke is therefore drawing our attention to the new situation which obtains for the Church once Jesus is in the presence of the Father, to the source of that prophetic fire which irrupts not just at Pentecost but in every moment of its existence into the organizational, institutional life of the Christian community and which Paul tells us must not be quenched by it. It is interesting to note that only once in his correspondence does Paul refer to an Ascension as distinct from the exaltation of the risen Lord, and then only with regard to the gifts of the Spirit exercised in the Church. In Ephesians 4.8, allowing himself some rabbinical licence, he uses a verse from the obscure sixty-eighth psalm to explain how Christ ascended far above all the concentric spheres in order to fill every corner of the cosmos with the victorious presence of his risen body and to send the Spirit upon the Church from which flow all gifts – prophetic, pastoral, administrative, didactic – for "the building up of the Body of Christ". The Ascension is therefore not so much an end for Christ as a beginning for the Church.

In Hebrews, which is close to the tradition in which Luke wrote, we find an extraordinarily rich treatment of the doctrine of the lordship and priesthood of the risen Christ. The Ascension is represented in this writing both as the accession to the throne ("ascending" the throne) of the king designate and the entering into the inner sanctuary by the Jewish high priest. In this way two of the most important forms which contemporary messianism took were combined in something of the way found in the Essene Damascus document which speaks of the messiah of Aaron and Israel.

One peculiarity of the treatment in Hebrews is, however, that it starts out from an interpretation of Psalm 110 which speaks of the priest-king like Melchisedek. This psalm, the *Dixit Dominus,* certainly had an important role in the earliest theological formulations as seen in the fact that it is quoted from or alluded to over a score of times in the New Testament. We know that these formulations came to expression within scriptural categories helped out by *testimonia* or lists of texts on a theme or point of teaching. Fragments of such lists have also been recovered at Qumran.

Psalm 110 evidently featured in the Christian *testimonia*. It begins with a divine oracle addressed to the king who is thought of as a priest-king like the Canaanite and Jebusite rulers dispossessed by the Hebrews, in particular Melchisedek, the Jerusalem priest-king whom some early Church writers went so far as to identify as a pre-incarnation of the Son of God. The right hand where he sits enthroned is the place of honour. It may refer to the special place in the temple reserved to the king of Judah in relation to the inner sanctuary where the invisible God was enthroned as king "upon the cherubim". What is implied, at any rate, is that the king rules as vice-regent for God. The Ascension therefore means that "the kingdom, the power and the glory" have been given by the Father to Jesus and that, as from the Resurrection, he rules by virtue of this absolute mandate whether in the Church where that rule is acknowledged or in the world where it is not. That this rule takes in all time and all space can be seen from the First Epistle of Peter which refers to him "who has gone into heaven and is at the right hand of God, with angels, authorities and powers subject to him". The consequence for our faith is therefore that we exist in a definite phase of history which begins with the enthronement of the risen Christ and ends with his coming from the throne in the royal *parousia* to judge and save.

In speaking of the risen Christ as priest, Hebrews develops the analogy of the great Day of Expiation (*yom kippur*) which was, in a way, the climax of all Jewish liturgy and religion. Just as the high priest, and he alone, entered into the Presence, by passing into the inner sanctuary through the veil, and that only once a year, so Jesus passes through the veil of heaven to perform the office of priestly mediation on behalf of the people. It is just here that we see how the Ascension is an integral part of the redemptive mystery. The self-offering of Jesus was through his acceptance of obedience to the Father to the point beyond which it is impossible to go – the point of death. But this offering had to be accepted, and the acceptance is shown in that he is now in the presence of the Father, "He entered once for all into the Holy Place . . . thus securing an eternal redemption" (Heb. 9.12). What he did was a "once-for-all" act (Heb. 7.27; 9.12, 26;

10.10, 12), "a single sacrifice for sins offered for all time" (10.12), which has opened the way for all those who, at any time, "draw near to God through him" (7.25).

We in the West have to a great extent lost this idea of our liturgy as a sharing in the heavenly liturgy of which Jesus present to the Father is the minister, *leitourgos* (Heb. 8.2). Yet in the great prayer of thanksgiving we ask that the gift offered be placed on the heavenly altar, we beg in the preface to the same prayer that we may unite our praise with that of the attendant angels, and throughout we pray to the Father "through Christ our Lord". In this respect Eastern liturgies have remained more faithful to that emphasis on communion with the ascended Lord which was so strong in the liturgical experience of the early Church. The Spirit which was manifested in freedom and power during the service (this is something which we have certainly lost) is that sent on the community from him. In fragments which have survived from early services, embedded in New Testament books, this idea is uppermost, as, for example, in the hymn in 1 Timothy 3.16 and the passage about the humiliation and exaltation of Christ in Philippians 2.6–11. This shows how necessary it is for us to reintegrate the Ascension into our theology of redemption and salvation.

The liturgical prayers of Ascension day speak mostly of hope and this is the final word since, in the last resort, the Ascension is a way of expressing the power of the risen Christ in the world and the fact that he alone is lord of history in spite of appearances to the contrary. To follow up an expression of Karl Barth, the game of chess goes on but black has lost already even if the defeat has not yet been acknowledged. This is the source from which springs all the force of renewal in the Church's life and mission now as at all times.

XIX

The Coming of Christ

THE COMING OF CHRIST in glory and the end of the world are represented in Christian doctrine as, respectively, the penultimate and ultimate stages of history and together form an idea which it is notoriously difficult for modern man to visualize or represent intelligibly to himself, let alone believe in. He does not *feel* it to be true. The world he knows is so different from that taken for granted by New Testament writers. There is in particular his enormously increased knowledge of the spatial dimensions of the world he lives in and the evolutionary timescale. The whole thing seems irrelevant. And even if we can talk about it intelligently in the kind of specialized language in use among theologians, does it really touch the life of the ordinary Christian? In other words, the difficulty is not just scientific, it is the way we feel about the world if we live in it at all. Teilhard de Chardin's assurance that the old earth will not fail us seems to make much better sense than all this talk about a fiery cancellation. In one of his letters Rilke puts this attitude into very succinct words:

> My feelings tell me that he *cannot* come. That there would be no sense in it. Our world is not just externally another world – it has no entrance for him.[1]

And for those of us who, unlike Rilke, have held on to some kind of faith, however tenuously, what does it mean to us as Advent comes round year after year and we listen to the eschatological discourse read in church and sing our hymns about the coming of our God?

The non-fulfilment of the glorious coming of Christ set a problem of faith right from the beginning, in a specially acute

[1] *Selected Letters of R. M. Rilke,* Macmillan, 1946, p. 338.

143

form once the first generation of Christians began to die off and nothing happened. We find an extreme form of this crisis in the words of the "scoffers" recorded in the Second Epistle of Peter:

> Where is now the promise of his coming? Our fathers have been laid to their rest, but still everything continues exactly as it always has been since the world began (2 Pet. 3.4).

Christians in Salonika were especially uneasy and had to be re-assured that their dear departed would not be absent from the rejoicings attendant on the glorious coming of Christ. Since the gospels form a deposit of the faith of the first generations and reflect their life, it is natural that we should find there many traces of this uneasiness, especially since they came into existence towards the end of the first generation. The complaint heard in the little story of the Neglectful Steward – "the Master is a long time coming!" – must have been on many lips at that time (Mt. 24.48). And still, after two thousand years, the Master has not come!

A first step towards understanding the biblical presentation of the coming of Christ and the end of the world is to penetrate as far as possible into the imagery under which they appear there and then try to reinterpret them in terms meaningful today. Taking individual expressions and metaphors one by one this can be fairly easily done. So, for example, we shall not feel obliged to interpret Joel 3.2, which speaks of a judgment to take place in the rather restricted space of the valley of Josaphat near Jerusalem, in the same way as those thousands of Jews who had themselves buried there in order to be on hand when the great day dawned. Most of what we find in the New Testament comes to us in the imagery and idiom of Jewish apocalyptic, not essentially different from what we find in other works of that time such as the Book of Jubilees or the Enoch literature. Divine judgment is generally expressed under the metaphor of fire as in the Old Testament prophets: the fire of a burning city, the track of a conquering and destroying army, the smouldering refuse of the Valley of Hinnom

(Gehennah). Beginning with the Sibylline Oracles, we find the world-end described as a cosmic bonfire and this is true also of the New Testament:

> By the word of God heavens existed long ago, and an earth formed out of water and by means of water, through which the world that then existed was deluged with water and perished. But by the same word the heavens and earth that now exist have been stored up for fire, being kept until the day of judgment and destruction of ungodly men (2 Pet. 3.5–7).

For the writer, the end consists in both cases in a return to the amorphous *materia prima* from which the world was understood (mistakenly) to be composed. It is therefore an act of uncreation, a return or reduction to the Chaos, the *tohu wabohu*, out of which God created in both cases. At the time of the composition of Genesis chapter 1 everyone, including the writer, supposed the world and its basic elements to be composed of an amorphous mass of water, a process which is undone step by step in the Flood, which was the end of *that* world. At the time of Christ, most people who thought of these things at all imagined the basic world-stuff to be fire. For the Stoics both the *anima mundi* and the *anima humana* were igneous. This is the view presupposed throughout the whole of the inter-testamentary period and therefore also by New Testament writers. It implies, among other things, that creation is not an absolute and irreversible datum; it depends on God and falls under his judgment; it is therefore precarious.

We may pause to note that the real possibility of discovering what *are* the basic constituents of the material world and of acting upon them has made it possible for man in our day to undo the tension which holds the cosmos together and thereby to initiate the process of uncreation. As Tillich put it, God has placed within man's reach the possibility of shaking the foundations. But in spite of the minatory language of judgment, the New Testament view of the end is of a fulfilment not a truncation, and one which is somehow present in the historical process and yet transcending it.

The coming of Christ which precedes the end is also spoken of in metaphorical terms. The starting-point is the climax of Daniel's vision of the four beasts, with the coming in the clouds of heaven of the one "like a man" to whom is given dominion and glory and kingdom (Dan. 7.13-14). Here again, this imagery of clouds opening, a throne and a royal accession to the throne, has to be penetrated and reinterpreted. When Christ himself told his accusers during his trial that they would see the Son of Man coming in the clouds of heaven this can hardly be understood in the visual sense unless we are to say that he was mistaken and deluded. It could mean simply that they would soon have absolutely clear proof of his messianic status. In the early correspondence of Paul we find the coming of the Lord described in terms of the royal *adventus,* the coming of the prince or emperor to a subject state or city, a royal visit in short, such as Vespasian paid to Alexandria when the people of the city went out to meet him with acclamations and brought him back in triumph to the city where, so we are told, he healed the sick and inaugurated an era of blessedness. This political metaphor is transparent in Paul's words to the Christians of Salonika:

> We who are alive, who are left, shall be caught up together with them (the dead) in the clouds to meet the Lord in the air (1 Thess. 4.17)

– not to remain "in the air", but to accompany him back to the earth, as the Alexandrians did Vespasian, where the era of messianic blessedness would be inaugurated. For what is promised is "new heavens and a new earth", a new created order to be set up on this earth where the history of God's act had begun.

This work of elucidating metaphor and imagery is an essential first stage but it still leaves us with the question with which we began: whether this is going to happen some day, whether an event like this is going to take place. The fact is that we find it difficult to think beyond our own particular *eschaton,* our death, when, as we suppose, the world is going to come to an end as far as *we* are concerned. That this is a real difficulty is shown by our traditional theology tending so strongly to individualize the teaching on the Last Things. What is primary is *my* death, *my* judgment, *my* prospect of hell or heaven. There is hardly any serious attempt to come to grips with the destiny of the whole created order and the human race within it. Leaving aside the question of whether we can detemporalize the end (or, for that matter, the beginning) as represented in the Scriptures, we can and must try to understand how the progressive Christian penetration of the Christ-event has profoundly modified the temporal element in Jewish eschatology. We should note, to begin with, how the redemptive event is seen in the New Testament as a unity, with the extension through stages of time practically ignored. So, in Paul's summary, there is only one underlying event – *God making all alive in Christ* – and the interim periods are ignored:

> As in Adam all die, so also in Christ shall all be made alive. But each in his own order: Christ the first fruits, then at his coming those who belong to Christ. Then comes the end, when he delivers the kingdom to God the Father after destroying every rule and every authority and power. For he must reign until he has put all his enemies under his feet. The last enemy to be destroyed is death (1 Cor. 15.22–26).

We are surely to understand the raising of the just in Jerusalem at the death of Christ as recorded in Matthew (27.52) and the raising of Lazarus in John (11) in the same way. They are more than a dramatic anticipation of the end. They show that the end is already somehow present.

This tension between the "already" and the "not yet", unique in Christian faith, finds its ultimate explanation in the mystery of Christ. He is the final and definitive self-revelation of God. In him God has said all that he will ever say. The meaning of the presence and activity of God is, we can say, exhausted in him. Therefore all that the end of the world means is already present in Christ since it is the word and the action of God which creates history. In him the dynamic of God's action comes to absolute completion. It follows that, since Christ is active in the Church, the Church must embody the last age of the world. All that the end of the world really means is experienced in the Church, since the Church is constituted by the sacraments and the Word and it is through these that the Christian already experiences what one New Testament theologian calls "the powers of the age to come" (Heb. 6.5).

In keeping with this, Christian life lived between the resurrection and the *parousia* is a working out in practice of this end which is already present in the middle of life. Hence its quality of challenge, crisis and decision. It is also an attempt to realize and appropriate that end in advance, which attempt gives the sense, the direction, to Christian effort. So Paul says, with reference to the risen Lord present in the Church, "We all, with unveiled face, beholding the glory of the Lord, *are being changed* into his likeness from one degree of glory to another" (2 Cor. 3.18). The Christians addressed in the Second Epistle of Peter are by their godly lives "waiting for and *hastening* the coming of the day of the Lord" (3.12). Since therefore the End is present the answer to the question When? recedes into the background, a process which can to some extent be traced throughout the New Testament writings, with the death of an increasing number of Christians, the realization of the magnitude of the missionary task facing the Church, the involvement of the whole of the natural order in this creative process of renewal which had to be carried through.

While the gospel reading for the first Mass of Christmas Day tells again the simple story of the marvellous Child, the lesson, which is taken from Paul's letter to Titus, sets before us the creative and redemptive act of God in its entirety, the act which took on visible form in the Child in the manger but which looks forward to "the happy fulfilment of our hopes when the splendour of our great God and saviour Christ Jesus will appear".